Christmas
with
Southern Living®
1989

**Compiled and Edited by
Kathleen English**

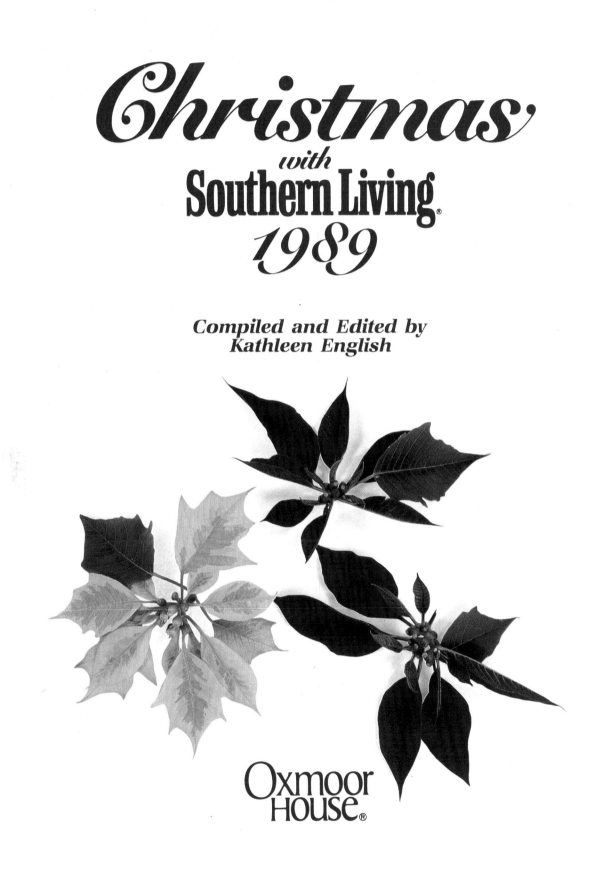

Oxmoor
House®

© 1989 by Oxmoor House, Inc.
Book Division of Southern Progress Corporation
P.O. Box 832463, Birmingham, Alabama 35201

Southern Living® is a federally registered trademark belonging to Southern Living, Inc.

Library of Congress Catalog Card Number: 84-63032
ISBN: 0-8487-0743-5
ISSN: 0747-7791
Manufactured in the United States of America
First Printing

Executive Editor: Nancy Janice Fitzpatrick
Production Manager: Jerry Higdon
Associate Production Manager: Rick Litton
Art Director: Bob Nance

Christmas with Southern Living 1989
Editor: Kathleen English
Assistant Editor: Margaret Allen Northen
Recipe Editors: Susan Payne, Associate Foods Editor, and Kaye Adams, Test Kitchens Director, *Southern Living*® magazine
Editorial Assistants: Karolyn Morgan, Alice London Cox
Production Assistant: Theresa L. Beste
Artists: Barbara Ball, David Morrison
Copy Chief: Mary Jean Haddin
Designer: Carol Middleton

To find out how you can order *Southern Living* magazine, write to *Southern Living*®, P.O. Box C-119, Birmingham, AL 35283

Introduction

Christmas around the South

Holiday Traditions

Contents

Introduction

Think of Christmas and the rush of images is dizzying. Jingling bells and bulging stockings. The scent of evergreens mixing with spices from the kitchen. A carload of loved ones who have traveled great distances to be with family. Such moments give shape to the holiday, and these pages reinforce that vitality.

In "Christmas around the South," you'll visit the world-famous Peabody ducks. "Holiday Traditions" gives you glimpses of how other Southerners celebrate, including a little boy whose birthday falls on Christmas Eve. In "Decorating for the Holidays," styles from country to formal present easy ideas you can adapt to your surroundings. Then, for handcrafted decorations and gifts, turn to "Christmas Bazaar." Whether you sew or saw, you'll find something to spur you into action. And speaking of action, some of the best during the holidays occurs in the kitchen. "Celebrations from the Kitchen" offers you delicious options, with all the cakes, pies, breads, and beverages a body could want.

While the meaning of the holiday lies within, your activities demonstrate its impact. Use this book to share your holiday spirit. And may Christmas 1989 be full of love, warmth, and beauty.

Christmas around the South

*E*mbark on an adventure back in time to see Southern holiday celebrations re-kindled. The roots of a candlelit Yule can be found in Old Salem with its Moravian traditions. And where two historic rivers meet—at Harpers Ferry—you'll encounter "Old Tyme Christmas." Bulloch Hall and the Peabody are steeped in timeless glamour, and a proud Fort Concho remembers its frontier past.

Recollections of a Yuletide Wedding

Three days before Christmas in 1853, Martha "Mittie" Bulloch married Theodore Roosevelt, Sr., at her family home in Roswell, Georgia. The house was trimmed with greenery and filled with family and friends. Tables were laden with hams, turkeys, cakes, and even ice cream, made with ice brought all the way from Savannah. As was the tradition at the time, the wedding was the focal point of two weeks of parties and gatherings.

Today Mittie's girlhood home is known as Bulloch Hall and is operated as a museum house. An excellent example of Greek Revival architecture, Bulloch is also historically important since Mittie and Theodore were the parents of our 26th president. Each December the Roswell Historic Preservation Commission presents "Christmas at Bulloch Hall," recalling that special Christmas of 1853. The house fills with people and the aroma of cooking. Music and laughter and festive decorations abound. There are specially decorated trees in every room, and costumed tour guides recount the history of the house and the Bulloch family. Local

Above: Bulloch Hall is located in Roswell, Georgia, about 20 miles north of Atlanta. The house was built in 1840 and is considered the finest example of Greek Revival architecture executed in wood and still standing in the Southeast.

Above: A performance by a group of young harpists is one example of the many musical entertainments offered during the Christmas season. The family parlor, with its tussie mussie tree and red mantel decorations, is a perfect backdrop for these talented girls.

Above: The aromas of fresh applesauce and homemade gingersnap cookies float through Bulloch, drawing crowds down to the basement kitchen. There, members of the Open Hearth Cooking Guild demonstrate the techniques of cooking in a beehive oven and at an open hearth. The kitchen tree is trimmed with simple ornaments, in keeping with the whitewashed walls and brick floors.

Above: The decorations in Mittie's bedroom reflect both the spirit of the season and the best of the Victorian era. The tabletop tree is decorated with bunches of dried flowers and accented with garlands of pink ribbon and ecru lace.

craftspeople fill the master bedroom with a wide range of gift items, including pepper jelly, quilts, and handmade dolls. Each day offers special entertainment events, ranging from choral and musical performances in the front parlor to open-hearth cooking demonstrations in the basement kitchen.

Members of the Open Hearth Cooking Guild, one of several craft guilds associated with Bulloch, conduct the cooking demonstrations. During the year, Bulloch is open for guided tours and available for private parties. Heritage Craft and Folk Art classes and craft guild meetings are held at Bulloch, as are special art and craft exhibitions.

The atmosphere at Bulloch is one of a peaceful, slower-paced life, when picnics were held on the banks of the nearby Chattahoochee River. Mittie always considered Roswell home and never forgot her Southern heritage, even though she lived in New York after her marriage. She often entertained her children with stories of her life in Roswell, where she grew up in the years before the Civil War. Mittie's soft voice and Southern speech enhanced her tales of a life far removed from that of her children. That life, with its simple elegance, is what infuses "Christmas at Bulloch Hall" with such contagious charm.

Savor Old Salem's Moravian Traditions

Christ the Lord,
the Lord most glorious,
Now is born;
O shout aloud!
Man by Him
is made victorious;
Praise your Savior,
hail your God!
—Moravian hymn

Above: This young boy, dressed in 18th-century Moravian attire, sits in front of a stack of freshly made lovefeast candles. During the early Moravians' lovefeasts and candle services, only children held the lit beeswax candles, but eventually the practice was extended to include candles for the adults, as well.

Small hands clutch flickering beeswax candles, ringed with red crepe paper ruffs. It's a renewing vision, the shifting candlelight reflected in young faces. At Home Moravian Church in Old Salem, North Carolina, this is Christmas Eve, and voices raised in song fill the sanctuary. The gathering is the annual children's lovefeast, and it's one of many beautiful and unusual events that take place during the holidays in Old Salem.

Toward the end of the ceremony, the lights dim, and candles are handed out to the children. As they sing the third verse of "Christ the Lord, the Lord Most Glorious," the children raise their candles high to symbolize Christ as the light of the world.

These young Moravians are carrying on a tradition that dates back to 1727, when their ancestors in Saxony, Germany, celebrated brotherhood and friendship by breaking bread together and singing hymns. The Moravians who settled Old Salem a few decades later brought the custom with them.

They established a carefully run, disciplined community and became a people known for the wide range of beautiful crafts they produced and their love of music. That legacy lives today in the restored community of Old Salem. Christmas decorations go up in Old Salem on December 1. During the

Above: The restored community of Old Salem forms a striking contrast to the modern city of Winston-Salem, with its towering skyscrapers.

Right and far right: In the silversmith shop of the John Vogler house, Dr. Ed Hill cuts a silhouette of an Old Salem hostess. Vogler was known for his hollow-cut silhouettes, and Dr. Hill carries on the practice at Christmastime today. A carved wooden gentleman holding a snuff box identifies the tobacco shop.

first two weekends of the month, the Women's Fellowship of Home Moravian Church holds candle teas in the Single Brothers' House (where unmarried men lived and learned their trades). There, members of the church share with visitors some of the rich history and religious traditions of the community.

Like the lovefeasts held in the church, the event includes singing of hymns and sharing of food. Visitors also see how the lovefeast candles are made. As each group enters the old dining room, they are met with the sweet aroma of melting beeswax. The women there string wicks through tin molds, pour the liquefied wax into the molds, and allow the candles to harden. They then remove the candles, trim them to standard sizes, and finish them with the traditional red ruffs, which are pretty and practical since they catch dripping wax.

Aromas lead the way again, as visitors go from the dining room to the kitchen. Costumed hosts and hostesses serve them the traditional Moravian sugar cake and a special coffee that has cream and sugar brewed into it. The last stop before leaving the Single Brothers' House is to see the beautiful *putz* (traditional German miniature scene) of the Nativity in the hills of Bethlehem and of the town of Salem as it looked in the 18th century. Many consider the candle teas the official beginning of the Christmas season.

The third weekend of the month brings the biggest event of the season—"Salem

Above: Traugott Bagge, Salem's first merchant, conducted his business from this building beginning in 1775. Old Salem, Inc., now operates a museum store here. Old Salem today is a fascinating mix of restored historic buildings open to the public and private residences. The result is a wonderfully preserved record of the past that is at the same time vital and thriving.

Opposite: Moravian bands perform during Old Salem's Christmas celebration, continuing the traditions of the early Moravians, for whom music was important. In the nearby Single Brothers' House, the Women's Fellowship of Home Moravian Church begins the Christmas season with candle teas. As visitors wait to participate in the candle teas, they can savor the sights and sounds of Old Salem along its well-traveled streets.

Christmas." This day-long celebration presents Salem as it was in its heyday, from 1790 to 1830. The streets and houses are decorated simply, with greenery, candles, and small amounts of ribbon. The many-pointed Moravian star is not much in evidence, since it appeared later than the period re-created for "Salem Christmas." But subtle as the decorations are, there is no lack of merriment connected with the season.

"Salem Christmas" is a festive day of special craft demonstrations, music indoors and outside, wagon rides, and cooking from another era. As many as 200 costumed people take part. From one end of Old Salem to the other, visitors can enjoy performances by bands, choral and instrumental ensembles, and individual players. Everywhere are the sounds of violins, flutes, horns, organs, and harpsichords.

The simple German people who tamed a wilderness didn't stop their work for excessive celebrations, even at Christmas. But in Old Salem today, visitors can see that nothing of the spirit or richness of the occasion has been lost as a result.

Above left: Dr. and Mrs. George Waynick, the current residents of the Kuehln house, have filled the house with Moravian antiques. Draped along the kitchen mantel are herbs and spices that the early Moravians would have used for both cooking and medicine.

Left: The living room mantel in the Kuehln house, built in 1831, demonstrates the early Moravians' craftsmanship. The silhouettes were cut by John Vogler.

Opposite: The dining room of the Kuehln house is decorated for the season with fruit and greenery. Spangling the swag on the mantel are Moravian Christmas cakes, actually thin ginger cookies, made with antique tin cookie cutters.

14

A Ducky Holiday In Memphis

As 11 a.m. approaches, the crowd in the lobby of the Peabody Hotel grows thicker. A 50-foot swath of red carpet flows from elevator doors to an elaborate travertine marble fountain, and people of all ages jockey for position along the crimson path. John Philip Sousa's "King Cotton March" booms over a public address system, the elevator doors part, and hundreds watch intently as the world-famous Peabody ducks begin their morning procession. They descend from their rooftop palace to spend the day frolicking in the fountain; then at 5 p.m. they ceremonially retire for the evening.

Though the fanfare is repeated twice each day throughout the year, in December, copious Christmas decorations make it even more spectacular. A 25-foot tree sparkles with over 2,000 lights; masses of flowers geyser from the carved fountain toward the skylights of hand-painted etched glass; and yards of garland festoon mezzanine railings.

Carolers from Memphis-area schools fill the lobby with the sounds of the season. Pastry chefs erect a life-sized gingerbread house modeled after a European-style pastry shop. And visitors to the elegant 64-year-old hotel nearly double in number, delighting in the performance of the ducks played out in this rich holiday setting.

Opposite: The magnificent lobby of the Peabody Hotel in Memphis, Tennessee, glitters for the season with thousands of tiny lights.

Above right and right: For over 50 years, the Peabody ducks have marched into and out of the lobby each day, frisking in the fountain from 11 a.m. to 5 p.m. The five mallards have a rooftop home for evening.

Rushing Rivers and a Blur of Time

Above: Visitors passing this group, in period dress for Olde Tyme Christmas, might have to blink to be sure they weren't seeing ghosts, especially considering the many sightings reported since Civil War days.

Harpers Ferry is a place of junctures and transitions. It's an old town, with worn brick and stone walkways, and it flows down the craggy West Virginia hillside to a point overlooking the confluence of the Shenandoah and Potomac rivers.

If you stand there, facing the rivers, you can see the adjoining states of Maryland, across the Potomac to the left, and Virginia, just over the ridge of hills to the right. As he watched the waters merge at that point 200 years ago, Thomas Jefferson remarked, "In the moment of their junction they rush together against the mountain, rend it asunder, and pass off to the sea. . . . This scene is worth a voyage across the Atlantic."

But less than a century later, devastation poured into this dramatically beautiful gorge, first in the person of John Brown, the firebrand abolitionist, and then with the Civil War. This complicated and rich heritage, which has stamped the town's identity, vividly comes to life during the two weekends of "Olde Tyme Christmas."

A section of Harpers Ferry became a national historic park in the forties, the preserved structures in the park commingling with the surrounding small community. In 1972, the townspeople and shop owners joined hands with the National Park Service to celebrate their history during the holidays. "Olde Tyme Christmas" began as a way to remember Christmas as it used to be—less hectic, full of good society and quiet religious celebrations. Word spread and the idea caught on. Now around 20,000 people visit Harpers Ferry each December.

The first two weekends of the month are filled with activities. On the first evening, the opening ceremony is the lighting of the yule log. Torches ignited from the log are carried in a procession along streets lined with luminarias. The glow spreads through the town as candles are lit from the torches.

This page: Nestled into the hills overlooking the confluence of the Shenandoah and Potomac rivers, Harpers Ferry, West Virginia, has seen both tranquility and strife in its long history.

Right: During Harpers Ferry Olde Tyme Christmas, a procession carrying "President Lincoln" travels down Shenandoah Street.

Below right: The Civil War, with the mixed loyalties it aroused, flavors much of the present-day experience of visiting Harpers Ferry.

Below: Quaint rows of shops, simply decorated, line the streets of this beautifully restored town.

St. Peter's Catholic Church, built in the 1830s and in continuous use since, presents a living nativity and several musical events. On Potomac Street, visitors can join in the world's biggest taffy pull, certified by none other than the *Guinness Book of World Records*, and observe a wreath-making demonstration using herbs and dried flowers.

Turn any corner and you're likely to run into a group of people, including soldiers from the Civil War, who appear to have stepped out of the 19th century. In what seems a dazzling display of time travel, "President Lincoln" arrives for the holidays in a horse-drawn procession.

Each Saturday and Sunday at dusk, luminarias are lit throughout the town, setting just the right mood for the highly popular ghost tours. So much blood was shed in and around Harpers Ferry, first with John Brown's ill-fated raid and later through the many battles for control of the town during the Civil War, that a spate of supernatural tales ensued. But for the easily frightened, other historical tours are available.

Carolers stroll the streets, hay rides transport old and young alike along the rows of decorated buildings, and kids romp through a peanuts-in-the-hay game and a pie-eating contest.

Betweentimes, visitors can pull out gift lists and visit the gaily decked shops with their wide range of offerings. Crafts, sweets, antiques, toys, and books are but a few of the items to browse among. And for those interested in the events that first brought Harpers Ferry to national attention, there's the John Brown Wax Museum.

Above right: Harpers Ferry boasts the world's largest taffy pull, listed in the Guinness Book of World Records. *The cooling taffy is a real test of strength for these two participants.*

Right: This craftswoman demonstrates the use of dried flowers and herbs to make beautiful holiday wreaths.

Deep in the Heart of Christmas

This page, top to bottom: Fort Concho, a 23-acre National Historic Landmark, is considered the best-preserved Indian wars fort in the nation. The six-man cavalry squad portrays Company D of the 4th Regiment, a unit stationed at Fort Concho from 1871 to 1873. This lady, dressed in holiday garb, is decorating a tree in one of the 22 historic buildings at Fort Concho.

In the heart of San Angelo, deep in the ranching country of West Texas, lies Old Fort Concho. The fort was established as a cavalry and infantry outpost in 1867 during the Indian wars of the post-Civil War era; today it is a National Historic Landmark and memorial to West Texas's frontier past.

Christmas is especially nostalgic at Fort Concho. It summons memories, not just of joyous days, but of harder times when distances were long and soldiers were far from home. Proud of this history, the people of San Angelo eagerly share it with visitors during "Christmas at Old Fort Concho," a traditional holiday celebration, which is observed the first weekend after Thanksgiving.

Attractions throughout the weekend include a heritage pageant with 200 costumed players, more than 100 merchants and artisans selling their wares, and programs of madrigals and carols.

In addition, strolling mariachis (Mexican street bands), children's choirs, ethnic dancers, and carriage rides provide lively entertainment. And visitors of all ages can experience moving observances of the first Christmas, such as a living nativity scene and a *posada* (a 300-year-old Mexican custom of re-enacting the Holy Family's journey to find a room in a Bethlehem inn).

Musket fire blasts as spectators witness historic battle re-creations performed by local residents. Dedicated to following correct military rank and procedure, these men, who call their group the Fort Concho Infantry, portray the 16th U.S. Infantry of the 1870s and 1880s and, like the cavalry squad (see photograph), wear replicas of uniforms of those times.

The proceeds from "Christmas at Old Fort Concho" go to the Fort Concho Museum for education, preservation, restoration, and special programs.

Holiday Traditions

*S*entimental bonds last a lifetime. Though silent and deep, they show themselves in hallowed customs, especially at Christmastime. Southerners cherish these customs, using them to celebrate their heritage and pass the scepter to a younger generation. This chapter shares traditions that capture the essence of Southern homecomings. Relish a gathering of old friends, visit a children's bazaar, and revel in the splendor of one of the country's finest mansions. Our offerings are sure to make your traditions even more special.

Tree-Trimming at Huckleberry Inn

Approaching the holidays as a newly married couple, Michael and Carolyn Cavanaugh soon realized they had a problem. Michael had come from a quietly religious family who celebrated the season in an understated way. Carolyn came from a large family who sought each year to outdo the merriment of the previous holiday season.

Love often begets creative compromise, and in the Cavanaughs' case, it led to the beginning of High and Low Christmasses and Friends' Christmas.

From year to year, Michael and Carolyn alternate between Low Christmas—a quiet, peaceful, reverent holiday—and High Christmas, filled with lavish decorations and joyful activities. One of these activities is

Above: Michael and Carolyn Cavanaugh welcomed friends at these steps for the first Friends' Christmas almost 19 years ago. Since then, they've made the house a bed-and-breakfast and painted it Homer's-tongue pink. (Homer is pictured in the foreground.)

Each of the friends who gathered for "Tree-Trimming at Huckleberry Inn" brought a favorite ornament to lend for the occasion. A different story came out with each ornament, and eventually both the Christmas tree and the hearts of those gathered around it were full.

Above and right: At dusk, the fully decorated 1915 structure shimmers with but a hint of the warmth it holds inside. Huckleberry Inn has operated as a bed-and-breakfast since 1986, but every other Christmas, it's the site of a joyous reunion. Over the years, Friends' Christmas has gradually grown in scope and structure to become the event pictured on these pages.

Friends' Christmas, a gathering that began almost 19 years ago as a way for young friends moving different directions in the world to keep in touch.

"Friends' Christmas has always been a celebration of joy and a celebration of bonds stretching over time and distance," says Michael. Carolyn adds, "These are friends who have touched each others' lives in significant ways, so when we celebrate together we celebrate not just an occasion but an ongoing spirit of togetherness."

The setting for the most recent Friends' Christmas was Huckleberry Inn, Michael and Carolyn's bed-and-breakfast in Leesville, Louisiana. The house has been in Michael's family since his grandparents built it in 1915. In the early years of Michael and Carolyn's marriage they lived in the house. In fact, they held the first Friends' Christmas there. After they moved to Baton Rouge, they hosted the celebrations in their "city home," but recent renovations to the inn made it a perfect place for the friends to gather again.

Each gathering has a theme, and the celebration pictured here was "Tree-Trimming at Huckleberry Inn." It began with the selection of a tree from the Christmas tree lot next door. Then the merry band spent the day making garlands and wreaths and hanging them inside and out at the inn.

Delicious Louisiana dishes kept the group fueled for each new challenge—treats such as Chicken-Sausage Jambalaya, Crawfish Pie, Bread Pudding, Sassafras Tea, and Aunt Jo's Praline Prizewinner Recipe.

That evening, freshened up and ready for more, the group gathered to trim the tree. Everyone had brought an ornament that held some significance to lend for the day, and as they hung the ornaments, they shared the accompanying stories.

More food followed the trimming, and fireside singalongs followed that, until the hour arrived to bid each other good-night. And sated with love and companionship enough to last two more years, the group left the next morning to resume their separate but linked lives.

Above: In keeping with the decorating theme of the year, Charlotte Elkins and Christy Barnes use materials gathered on the grounds to make wreaths that reflect the styles of the various rooms of Huckleberry Inn.

Top: Carolyn Cavanaugh brings up the rear as her friends Lloyd Frye and Jeff Floyd drag away the tree they've selected from the Christmas tree farm adjacent to Huckleberry Inn. In an admirable display of democracy, the group surveyed the five acres of trees, gave speeches to each other—lobbying for favorites, and voted to choose the one that would grace the living room of Huckleberry Inn.

Imaginative Children Stage a Holiday Bazaar

When Carol Tipton's children, Andy, Ryan, and Sarah, wanted to earn money for Christmas shopping, she suggested they make some craft items and set up a Christmas bazaar to sell them. Carol invited two of the children's playmates, Matthew and Charlotte Deason, and their mother, Genie, to join in the fun. Since the children are ages 2½ to 6½, Carol and Genie carefully planned a variety of craft projects for them and advanced them money to buy supplies.

The first workday, the children assembled wooden jigsaw puzzles, stuffed cloth dolls, strung spools into necklaces, and made birdseed ornaments. On a second workday, they increased their inventory to include craft-stick bookmarks and tiny candles in decorated spool holders.

Then, in early December, family and friends were invited to the Tiptons' house to buy the one-of-a-kind, perfect for gift-giving crafts. The children acted as salespeople, taking customers by the hand and showing off their wares. Carol and Genie contributed Christmas decorations and hot cider to the event. The children even made a poppyseed cake to serve their guests.

"The bazaar was a fun learning experience for all of us. In fact, the children enjoyed it so much they're still selling things—to each other," Carol says. Sarah, the littlest entrepreneur, spent her share of the profits on gloves for her brothers. "The children are so proud to have earned their own money that they've already started planning for next year," chuckles Carol.

Left: While Matthew, Ryan, and Andy draw more animals and people, Sarah and Charlotte stuff the almost-finished dolls. Dinosaurs, cowboys, and ballerinas are just a few of the subjects chosen by the children for these one-of-a-kind dolls.

FANCIFUL DOLLS

First, have the child draw a picture on white paper with fabric crayons. Carol recommends that the children draw pictures without a background or words. Transfer the drawing to white fabric with an iron. Cut out the picture, following the outline of the subject and adding seam allowance; then back it with a colorful scrap print, leaving an opening for turning and stuffing. Stuff firmly and sew the opening closed.

Above: A spool necklace is a wonderful accessory to a little girl's wardrobe. Charlotte and Sarah carefully select wooden spools and beads to string on colorful satin ribbons. Painted spools and beads or large buttons could be used for another touch of color.

Above left: Carol cuts a puzzle into pieces on the jigsaw, while Matthew, Ryan, and Andy carefully sand the cut pieces. When all the pieces are thoroughly sanded, the boys put them in a plastic bag tied with a bright red ribbon. To make these small puzzles, the children glued Christmas card pictures to pieces of ¼" wood.

Left: Amid cries of "Buy from me!" shoppers at the children's bazaar begin to browse. Grandmother is a very willing shopper—the only dilemma is which doll to choose. Charlotte points out the subtle details of a dinosaur doll, while Matthew and Andy look on in anticipation of a big sale. Naturally, Grandmother purchased items from each of the children.

Biltmore Estate: Decorating On a Grand Scale

On December 25, 1895, the *Asheville Citizen* reported a major event: "The hearth fires in Biltmore House yesterday cracked a cheery Christmas warming to members of George W. Vanderbilt's family who came from the North to honor the occasion."

On 125,000 acres of rolling western North Carolina countryside, over 1,000 workmen had labored for five years to erect the mansion and sculpt the gardens of Biltmore Estate. On Christmas Eve, the young Vanderbilt opened his new home to the public for the first time. Today's celebrations at Biltmore Estate reflect the grandeur of that first Victorian Christmas.

When Cathy Barnhardt, a horticulturist and landscape designer, went to work at Biltmore 12 years ago, she was put in charge of the holiday decorations.

"They had decorated the house only once in recent years, and then only on a limited

Above right: In the hills of western North Carolina, George Vanderbilt chose this location for his country estate not only because of its beauty, but also because it so well suited the experiments he wanted to conduct in agriculture, forestry, and stockbreeding.

Right: Though Cathy Barnhardt is a horticulturist by training, her duties as holiday decorator at Biltmore Estate have taken her off on a whole new tack. She has researched Victorian decorations carefully and learned to reproduce them in her workshop.

Opposite: This second floor living hall was the Vanderbilt family parlor. Each year, the hall is decorated for Christmas much as it might have been in the late 19th century, featuring Cathy Barnhardt's handmade feather wreaths, tussie mussies, and other ornaments.

basis," she says. "I started looking for information on Victorian decorations, but there wasn't much out at that time."

Cathy began by looking in Biltmore's massive library and archives. George W. Vanderbilt was a scholar who spoke eight languages. He compiled a library containing over 20,000 volumes, and among them, Cathy found a booklet of napkin folds and magazines describing handmade ornaments from the 19th century.

She learned even more from libraries and other museum houses of the period. But her creations go beyond the history she has uncovered. "We can't know exactly what the Vanderbilts did to decorate. We try to be as authentic as possible. We use a lot of fresh greenery—cartloads of holly and other things mentioned in newspaper accounts of the day—and we use ribbons and beads as they did. But we really have to just use our imaginations. I'm sure whoever did the decorations then did that."

From Cathy's imagination come tiny feather wreaths and pomander balls sheathed in tulle and crowned by loops of ribbon and bits of dried flowers. She fills real ice cream cones with potpourri-covered balls and makes camellias from white crepe paper and fans from glittering gift wrap.

And when holiday visitors arrive, seeing these treasures on over 20 trees, they can imagine that Christmas Eve in 1895 when George Vanderbilt proudly presented his home to family and friends.

Above left: Tussie mussies were extremely popular in Victorian times. Ladies carried them in hand, placed them on tables, and tucked them into arrangements. This one is made of silk roses, dried flowers, a paper doily, and generous loops of ribbon.

Left: The Victorians created their decorations using natural materials combined with ribbons, beads, and lace. Feathers were plentiful and popular, and cut into small lengths, they made beautiful, tiny wreath ornaments like these.

Left: Cathy found this napkin fold illustrated in a Victorian-era book she came across in the Biltmore library. The perky elf shoe fold is a favorite among holiday visitors to the mansion. See below for directions.

ELF SHOE NAPKIN FOLD

This fold will work with a paper or starched linen napkin. If shoe will be used for decoration only, use a 5" square of aluminum foil to hold curl in toe. Omit foil if shoe is to be used as a dinner napkin. Press all folds as they are made.

Place the foil in the center of the napkin. Fold napkin from bottom to top twice, following Diagram 1. Fold down corners (A and B) to meet in center, creating a point. (See Diagram 2.)

Fold in upper sides (C and D) as shown in Diagram 3, to meet in center.

Fold napkin down center to create "paper airplane." Hold in left hand, with point to left and fold on top, as shown in Diagram 4. Follow Diagram 5 to fold the flap (E) nearest you up to the left, and then tuck the other flap (F) into the slit pocket on the side of the boot nearest you. If napkin is large, fold collar opening down. Turn toe up to curl.

Embellish with ribbon and trims as desired. If used as a dinner napkin, shoe can hold party favors.

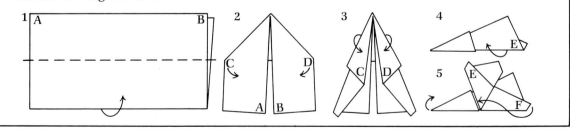

A Creative Legacy In North Carolina

Above: Starting with the entry, Lorraine Erwin displays objects from her collections all through her house, and each treasure has a story she loves to tell.

Atop a South Carolina pie safe, Lorraine Erwin's carved and painted wooden Santas congregate with other merry old gents from her collection. Lorraine is a craftswoman—quilter, woodworker, painter—and her talents are gloriously in evidence at Christmastime. Feathers, flowers, herbs, and twigs sprout from her holiday decorations. And her beautifully detailed quilts adorn pie safe doors and sofas, in addition to warming toes in bed.

In her workshop, she cuts away wood to reveal Santas, bunnies, hearts, and swans. She carves and paints them, in a beautiful folk art style all her own, and displays them with the other folk art pieces she collects—North Carolina salt-glaze pottery, decoys, antique furniture, and miniatures. In winter, when the workshop is chilly, she switches to quilting.

Her creativity stems from a rich heritage; the family's legacy thrives now in three generations. According to Lorraine, her father, John Mitzel, can do anything with tools and metal. "I wanted him to get into my kind of thing, so I said, 'Daddy, how about cutting little hearts out of tin?' and he said, 'Sure, give me a pattern.' I drew one and he came down a few days later with some little tin hearts."

At her request, her father has contributed all sorts of tiny pieces to her collection of miniatures—despite the fact that he has very large hands. Lorraine can't hold back a chuckle when she remembers that he once told a friend, "I do wish Lorraine would think bigger."

Her mother, Margaret, is a retired kindergarten teacher who now makes paper cutouts for patients at the local hospital. And Lorraine's children carry on the tradition. Caren is her oldest daughter and the mother of two. Caren's specialty is delicate *scherenschnitte* (cut paper) pieces that she

Above: Lorraine's father planned to use the old ice cream table and chairs he found for his metal work, but Lorraine begged them away. Her repainting included a chessboard on the tabletop. The sign hanging over the chest is an authentic English tavern sign.

Above: The decorations on this pie safe represent the range of Lorraine's craft skills. Over one door is a quilt of hers with a heart motif. On top, with pieces she's collected, are her Santa (on horseback at right) and little tree (beside fireplace).

antiques. The younger daughter, Marsie, cross-stitches samplers that Lorraine displays in stenciled frames of her own design.

Those samplers, Lorraine's wood carvings and stitched pieces, and other handcrafted items are then put up for sale in her shop in the Cubbyhole. (Its name comes from the fact that it's a co-op, with eight vendors operating out of the store—all have their own little cubbyholes.)

"This past Christmas was my first one in retail," Lorraine recalls. "You know, you're not through until Christmas Eve. I think Bill [her husband] was wondering if I was going to decorate the house or not. One night he came home with about a dozen poinsettias and banked them along the stairs."

Bill's support has spanned the years since Lorraine was a young housewife who made the presents the family gave each year. She has progressed to become an artist who sells to designers and retailers, and now, into becoming a retailer herself.

But professional involvements haven't changed the way she celebrates the season, even if her decorating time is cut short. The Erwin family enjoys her beautiful handmade Santas and sleighs, quilts and miniature trees from one end of the house to the other. For instructions on Lorraine's folk art sleigh and her heart and bunny napkin rings, turn to page 80.

A Doll Tree

Remember the childhood excitement of tearing open a special Christmas gift? That is a memory that Marcia Harris of San Antonio, Texas, savors. "I grew up during World War II, and gifts were scarce, even for the children. But I was always delighted when I saw that my gift was in a shiny white box with pink or red polka dots!" She recognized that box as containing a porcelain Storybook doll, clad in a crisp, colorful dress.

In all, Marcia collected between 25 and 30 of the original dolls, which had bendable legs so that they could be displayed either standing or seated.

Marcia recalls that the porcelain beauties always stayed safely tucked high on a bedroom shelf. "Can you imagine being a young girl with a cherished collection of dolls and *not* being able to play with them?!"

In time she became thankful for her parents' foresight, and when she married, she, too, packed the dolls away—this time in the attic—for safekeeping.

That's where they stayed until a few years ago when Marcia was showing her prized collection to a friend, who suggested that Marcia display it for all to admire.

The result of that conversation can be seen in the dining room of Marcia's home every Christmas. With pipe cleaners, she carefully anchors the dolls to the branches of a sturdy Noble fir, and in keeping with the nostalgic theme of the tree, she adds strands of pearls, heirloom ornaments, and twinkling candles.

Since that first year, decorating the doll tree has become a part of Marcia's holiday ritual. She places the tree in the dining room, between the doorways to the sunroom and living room, where it can be enjoyed from several spots. She encourages anyone with a special childhood collection to incorporate it into her home—especially at Christmas when the festive celebrations evoke heartwarming memories.

A Birthday Tree

Colin Woodworth's mom has noticed that he frequently, if not quietly, enjoys the party blowers on his tree. She's very tolerant, however, of the sometimes startling honks and whistles. You see, Colin's birthday is Christmas Eve, but he's far from being one of the unfortunates whose birthdays get lost in the holiday shuffle.

Colin's mom, Claudette, uses her skills as a craft designer to draw a careful distinction between birthday and holiday, even while cleverly merging the two events. Colin has his own tree, right by the front door, decorated by and for him.

His collection of stuffed animals congregates around the base, and a birthday hat and a large number proclaiming the age he will turn form the topper. Amassed in between are ornaments and birthday paraphernalia in profusion. They include decorations he and his older brother have made, shower presents Claudette received when she was expecting Colin, egg ornaments crafted by a friend, and a popcorn garland strung by the birthday boy himself.

Then there are the animal ornaments. You could say Colin is wild about animals. At the zoo, in his hometown of Baltimore, Colin has adopted a boa constrictor and a bear. "It's like a black bear," Colin explained, "and its stomach is brown. He loves to roll around." Claudette says Colin has had a garter snake, hamsters, guinea pigs, and cicadas, which he learned to appreciate in science class. Most recently he's taken up cats. Four of them.

It naturally follows that along the limbs of his tree, among the birthday decorations, various members of the animal kingdom roam. Which ornament is his favorite? He says he likes Snoopy best, but Claudette thinks he really prefers the party blowers. At least from the sound of things.

To see more of Claudette's holiday decorations, turn to page 44.

Above: The mantel in Sunny's living room is draped with a graceful garland that was inspired by a trip to Europe a few years ago. She used silk flowers, painted pinecones, and sweet gum balls and walnuts wrapped in gold to achieve an old-world Victorian ambience.

First Lady of Victoriana

When you enter her turn-of-the-century farmhouse in Bethesda, Maryland, it's easy to see why Sunny O'Neil is known as the First Lady of Victoriana. Genteel crafts and furnishings line the walls.

Widely recognized as an authority on Victoriana, Sunny conducts classes at the Smithsonian Institution. She has decorated trees for the "Trees for Christmas" exhibit, and she wrote *The Gift of Christmas Past*, which is an excellent holiday sourcebook for Victorian traditions.

Every year at Christmastime, she leads tours through her home. In her shop, she demonstrates her skills with pressed and dried flowers and sells the supplies so that others can fashion their own treasures.

Sunny's interest in Victorian Christmas traditions has evolved over the years into a full-time avocation. And, for those who share her desire to re-create the spirit of an old-fashioned Christmas, Sunny continues to be a source of inspiration.

Left: Sunny glued dried flowers on this small artificial Christmas tree. (She pulled out the branches on one side so that it would fit against the wall.) A red paper bow at the bottom provides the perfect finishing touch.

Decorating for the Holidays

When it comes to creating a warm, welcoming atmosphere for friends and family, your Christmas decorations say it all. They form a loving backdrop for the upcoming festivities and create many a visitor's lingering impressions of your home. In the following pages, we include tempting ideas that you can add to your decorating palette this year. Try using the luscious fruit of winter in distinctive ways, finding exciting new spots for traditional poinsettias, and creating exquisite table and door decorations and package toppers. So, get ready to be inspired: this chapter will help you establish your creative niche for the season.

Celebrate with Nature's Bounty

Ours is a lush, blooming region, offering a wealth of colorful natural material, even in deepest winter. Fruits and berries, greenery and cones—these form the palette for the decorations shown here.

Over a mantel, an enormous boxwood wreath is sprinkled with apples, walnuts, pinecones, arborvitae berries, and nandina berries. Decorative pineapples anchor the bottom, while a raffia bow adorns the top.

The theme continues throughout the house, with baskets and bowls cradling masses of fruit, berries, and greenery. A thick boxwood garland along the banister

Left and above: Fat and thin, standing and seated, a lineup of Santa suspects on this mantel illustrates the elusive character of the merry old man. There's nothing elusive about a wreath wrought from nature, though. It's a perfect place for the jolly gents to gather.

39

features bunches of apples at the rise of each swag. The apples are grouped with magnolia leaves and berries and then firmly wired in place. To minimize discoloration where the wire punctures the fruit, a bit of lemon juice is dabbed on each hole.

Bushel baskets filled with fruit and vegetables provide an element of surprise in such a grand setting. Kale, grapes, apples, and pomegranates become a grouping that holds the eye. Pinecones add to the feeling of sheer volume, and together with the collection of baskets, add contrasting texture.

Across the foyer, the arrangement is repeated with a basket holding fruit, berries, and a new addition—cinnamon sticks. The combination of cinnamon and fruit decorates with scent as well as color.

On tabletops, mantels, and stairways, fruit and greenery are as dramatic as the shiniest ribbon and brightest lights. And an extra bonus is that, with decorations like these, cooks will never come up an apple short in the kitchen!

Above left: A crystal bowl laden with fruit and greens sets the tone in this room. Christmas pillows offer a holiday invitation from the couch, while outside, a topiary reindeer seems to graze happily in winter verdure.

Left: Bushels of beauty fill the foyer below a grand staircase. Along the banister, fresh greenery sprouts clusters of apples topped with tapestry bows. The boxwood garland spills to the floor, and behind it, baskets of apples, grapes, kale, and pomegranates suggest the largess of an old-world vegetable market.

Opposite: A sheaf of cinnamon sticks is caught about its middle with a tapestry tie. Vines dotted with winter berries of various hues and types swirl into the air and twist around the cinnamon sticks and basket. A few pieces of fruit pool at the base of the arrangement, repeating the stairway decorations just across the foyer.

The Allure Of Poinsettias

Picturesque poinsettias abound this time of year. And it's no wonder. They are stunning, filling your home with holiday spirit.

To decorate with these versatile plants, look for a location in which the poinsettias, with their beautifully colored bracts and tiny yellow flowers, will mingle with your other decorations. Bank them in masses on a stairway, or tuck them in a spot that deserves some extra attention.

Once you've determined the site, select from an array of colors. White bracts traditionally suggest formality, while red and pink are more festive. But opt for hues to suit your preference and decor.

Then be creative with bows, candles, and greenery accents. The unexpected can produce magnificent results.

Above left: This poinsettia tree features 12 four-inch plants. A tomato cage, set in a plastic container, holds florists' foam. The roots of each plant (still in soil) and two teaspoons of water are tied in plastic bags, and the bracts are then wired to the cage in a spiral pattern. With florists' foam stacked behind for support and moisture, greenery, Spanish moss, and Chinese tallow fill out the tree.

Bottom left: A blaze of scarlet poinsettias is placed under this glass-top table to stay out of the way of holiday hustle and bustle. The colorful plants and the brass accessories on the table create an effective contrast.

Opposite: A waterfall of pink poinsettias requires only a ripple of greenery to avoid rivalry between elements. Artfully pruned poinsettia standards (shown on the landing and at the bottom of the stairs) can be purchased at a local nursery. Or, ask your nurseryman for advice on cultivating them in your region.

Stylish Flourishes Set This House Apart

Just outside Baltimore, Claudette Woodworth is putting the finishing touches on decorations in her 1850s home. A crafts designer, Claudette finds the task rewarding on many levels. Her son Colin was a Christmas Eve baby (see story on page 35), and she enjoys the challenge of decorating to celebrate two very special days.

She fills her home with trees—large and small, bright and subdued—all adding scents of the season to the rooms they embellish. In addition to Colin's birthday tree, Claudette has a tree in her living room that she decorates to her taste one year and to her children's the next.

"The boys prefer a red and green tree, so I alternate," Claudette says, adjusting the swirling ribbon on the tree. But it's her turn, and she's chosen gold lamé, feathers, and iridescent ribbon. Against a brick floor and neutral backdrop, the effect is striking.

The house offers many features like the brick floor for inspiration. "This house was originally a two-room tenant farmer's home," Claudette explains. "Through the years the people who've lived here have added on, but they were always sensitive to the house's original proportions."

The brick floor was installed by an artist, who also left behind several stained glass windows. After a local historical preservationist lived here, he bequeathed future owners his finely crafted built-in bookcases.

Claudette's kitchen, like most, is a popular spot, and she has placed some of her cleverest decorations there. She believes in combining favorite pieces she's collected with simple naturals—baby's breath, pine branches, pinecones—and then adding a bit of sparkle here and there. In these festive rooms, there's something for everybody, even the birthday boy.

Above: Since it's Claudette's turn to decorate the living room tree, she chooses satin balls wrapped in gold lamé, white lights, and a white feather boa garland to give the tree glitzy style.

Opposite: With an artist's eye, Claudette begins with a collection of baskets, a straw hat, pieces of lace, and a coverlet and then adds pine branches, pinecones, and canella berries to bring seasonal dash to this tabletop. The mix of textures and subtle use of color are what make the arrangement so effective.

Right: Even the kitchen hutch is decorated for the season. Claudette drapes pieces of lace along shelves and under crockery. She banks pine along the top of the hutch and sprinkles baby's breath and foil-wrapped chocolate money along the boughs. Fat white candles are tied with gold ribbon, and cinnamon sticks are caught with ribbon, baby's breath, and canella berries. And the spices, legumes, and utensils are still handy!

Above: A little countertop tree is decorated with ornaments fitting the location: bouquets garnis (spice mixtures for cooking, tied in cheesecloth bags) and foil-covered chocolate money, kissed with tiny bows, hang from diminutive branches. At the ready for drop-in company are mugs containing napkins and cinnamon stick stirrers and a bowl filled with a coffee and cocoa mixture. Pine branches, pinecones, and berries repeat the decorations on the hutch and kitchen table.

46

Above: Claudette's kitchen table demonstrates how simple elements can pack a powerful decorating punch. Her rag runner is centered with a basket that has painted wooden apples clustered on each side. A mass of baby's breath fills it to its handle, and pine branches stretch out from the basket, lightly carpeting the length of the runner. Adding height and texture are spool candle holders and pinecones.

Sparkling Shapes from Sugarplums

Sweets of the season do decorative double duty with these creations from gumdrops. A sugarplum theme gives Christmas dishes a festive appeal, and taking it one step further by fashioning table decorations with the candies adds professional polish. Accolades for the clever hostess can only follow.

A gumdrop-and-boxwood tree designed to look like a standard (an upright, pruned tree) takes a formal design and makes it playful with slivers of swirling ribbon and a candy-striped "trunk." White cupcakes wear sugary sprigs of holly. Gumdrop roses become a singular nosegay, and others cluster atop a coconut cake. Some of the confectionary concoctions are edible; others are simply pretty; but all are easy to make. Instructions for the gumdrop roses and holly are on the next page.

For the gumdrop tree, push a craft-foam ball 2″ in diameter onto a 5½″-long piece of ³/₁₆″ dowel. Spiral red curling ribbon down the dowel and glue it at both ends. Cut a piece of heavy cardboard in a circle large enough to cover the bottom of the terracotta pot, and fill the pot with pebbles to hold the tree upright. Mount gumdrops on toothpicks and insert them evenly over the ball; then fill in with sprigs of boxwood. Split red ribbon into thin strips and curl it on scissors; then swirl over the surface.

More strips of the ribbon, threaded through cupcake liners with a tapestry needle, tie the cupcakes into the setting. On a little wrapped party favor, a gumdrop sliced in half fills in as the bow's knot. Once you explore the candy's possibilities, more ideas

Above: The sweetest nosegay is made from gumdrop roses cupped in a doily and cinched with narrow red and green satin ribbon. Instructions for making the sugary flowers are on the next page.

Opposite: Sugarplums will dance in the heads of your guests long after they've sampled the cupcakes that sprout gumdrop holly sprigs. With a gumdrop theme, many decorations will be gobbled up, but some, like the boxwood tree, can last beyond a single event—just replace drooping greenery.

will occur. Try making small wreaths with craft-foam forms and the techniques and materials used for the tree.

Use the gumdrop tree as a single arrangement, or make several to hold place cards. Tiny trees, using smaller craft-foam balls and pots, would look enchanting supporting cards, with the names of your guests written in red and green ink.

To your guests, the sugarplum embellishments will appear lovingly conceived and whimsically executed. And isn't that what every party should be?

Above: Looking as though they've pushed their heads through a dusting of snow, these gumdrop roses add sparkle to a simple coconut cake. The confection becomes a decoration when it's displayed on a tapestry-covered stand next to a spray of elaeagnus and trailing ivy, of both the metallic and living varieties.

GUMDROP ROSES

Place desired-color gumdrop on flat end and cut into five pie-shaped pieces. Coat cut sides with granulated sugar and roll pieces out with a rolling pin as thin as possible to form petals. Use granulated sugar to keep them from sticking to the surface, but keep a little sticky for joining together later.

For the nosegay, cut a 7″ length of wire and bend a small hook in one end. Roll a petal around the hook into a cone shape to form center of rose. Take a small petal and wrap it around center, squeezing it at the bottom to stick to center. Curl back top edge.

Overlapping that petal, wrap another petal around rose, attaching and curling as for previous one. Continue adding petals until rose is desired fullness. Trim wire, if needed, and wrap with green florists' tape. Finish with a doily collar and ribbon.

For roses to place on a cake, omit the wire. To make green leaves, cut a gumdrop into six pieces. Roll out and shape them as for rose petals, trimming edges to shape. To intensify the green color, use granulated sugar dyed with food coloring.

GUMDROP HOLLY

Cut a green gumdrop into four pieces and roll out as for rose leaves, using granulated sugar dyed green. To make berries, cut a red gumdrop into quarters and slice each quarter into thirds. Roll berries in your fingers, dipping them in red-tinted granulated sugar.

50

All That Glitters

Introduce a brilliance to your holidays with lustrous gold, intertwined with green, in a distinctive entry decoration. Permanent greenery, adorned with shiny ribbon and natural ornaments, produces a simple and sophisticated treatment for a doorway.

Gold spray paint makes pods, magnolia leaves, gerbera daisies, and artichokes the surprises in this wreath. Bunches of grapes,

strands of beads, and an abundant, glittery ribbon bow with streamers, all wired securely to a full green wreath, complete the look. Ribbon, woven through evergreens in planters, reflects twinkling white lights after dark, finishing this elegant portal.

For a head start on next year, remove the perishables, which can be quickly replaced, and carefully pack the wreath away.

Peaches and Potpourri

The gentility of the past finds expression in these lacy peach-and-white decorations. Fashion them yourself—elegant nosegays of ribbon and dried flowers, lace fans caught with silk flowers, and rolled pieces of sheet music. These package toppers stay intact after gifts are unwrapped, becoming keepsake ornaments. To make the heart ornaments, bend a 12-inch length of wire into a heart shape and cut a piece of lace twice as long. Fold the lace in half lengthwise and run a gathering stitch along the open edge. Slide the lace over the wire, gathering it to fit, and tack the ends together. To finish, tack on a ribbon rose.

Dangling from the dining room chandelier are pinecones that have been coated with spray glue and then shaken in a bag of potpourri. Bows with a looped ribbon hanger are glued to the tops, and if the loops are stuffed with tissue before packing, the ornaments will last for seasons to come.

These pages: Crisp white paper striped with gloss, ribbon roses, yards of satin ribbon and lace, and bunches of dried flowers create presents that decorate this room until recipients lay claim to them. And after the gifts are unwrapped, the detachable toppers will be added to ornament collections. In the dining room, potpourri-covered pinecones become chandelier pendants, gently scenting the room.

Rag Doll Delights: Yarn Hair, Button Eyes, and Christmas Charm

Nestled on window ledges and propped in chairs, a party of rag dolls celebrates Christmas. Young, old, large, and small, their smiles evoke an era gone by. Yarn hair and black button eyes are the common denominators that make this group an irresistible collection.

This breakfast nook's holiday decor is enlivened by the play of color: the vivid red of the dolls' hair, the deep green of the walls, and the colorful prints of the fabrics.

The whimsical setting of the tea party table centers on a permanent tree, designed for the young at heart. Miniature books and toys, wrapped packages, candy canes, and holly leaves, in abundance, entice the viewer to come closer and look at every single prize. (To make a tabletop tree like this, simply coat a craft foam cone with spray glue; press Spanish moss over its surface; then hot-glue or wire trinkets in place.)

Cookies laden with icing and sprinkles, displayed on Christmas plates, and milk served in decorated glasses make a tempting holiday tea. It's an inviting scene. The children in this house better hurry or they may find mere crumbs left, as the rag dolls wipe their mouths and smile.

Christmas Bazaar

*P*ersonal style. Certain people have it. From the way they wrap a present to the way they display a group of candles, everything carries an individual stamp. If you're one of those people, you know that creating one-of-a-kind wraps, cards, decorations, and presents often takes more thought than time. Take the paper garland in this chapter. You can snip it in a wink—the choice of paper is the hardest part. But if you also enjoy the challenge of fine handiwork, you'll find that, as well.

A Ruffled Set Rings with Country Style

Reminiscent of an English country decor, green toile fabric trimmed in rose is a warm alternative to traditional Christmas colors. Ruffled edges and ribbon-tied bells adorn this tree skirt and stocking, which can be adapted to any holiday color scheme by simply substituting another ribbon color.

BELL STOCKING

Materials:
patterns on page 140
1¼ yards (45"-wide) green print fabric
¼ yard (45"-wide) cream-on-cream print fabric
thread to match
½ yard (45"-wide) thin quilt batting
½ yard (⅛"-wide) pink satin ribbon
¼ yard (¹⁄₁₆"-wide) pink satin ribbon
thread to match
⅝ yard (1"-wide) cream flat lace trim
4⅝ yards (¼"-wide) pink picot-edged ribbon

Note: Add ½" seam allowance to all pattern pieces.

Following pattern, extend stocking leg, transfer to fabric and batting, and cut out stocking front and back, 2 lining pieces, and 2 batting pieces. From green print, cut 5"-wide bias strips, piecing as needed, to make 1¼ yards for ruffle. Fold in half, long edges aligned and wrong sides facing; press. Sew a row of gathering stitches along raw edges.

Cut one 7" length of lace trim and 2 (7") lengths of ⅛"-wide ribbon. Stitch to toe of stocking front as shown on pattern.

Pin batting pieces to wrong sides of stocking front and back. With right sides facing, stitch front to back, leaving top open. Trim batting from seams, clip curves, and turn.

With right sides of stocking lining pieces facing, stitch, leaving top open. Clip curves. Do not turn.

Gather ruffle to fit around top of stocking. Stitch ruffle to right side of stocking with raw edges aligned. Slip lining over stocking, with right sides facing and raw edges aligned, and stitch top edge, leaving a 3" opening. Trim batting from seam and turn. Slide lining into stocking. Slipstitch closed.

Cut 1½" x 6" rectangle from green print for hanger. Fold 6" edges together, right sides facing, and stitch all around, leaving an opening to turn. Turn, press and whipstitch closed. Fold into a loop and tack to inside back of stocking.

Cut 4 bells from cream fabric and 2 from batting. Cut 2 (6") pieces of lace trim and 2 (4½") pieces of ¹⁄₁₆" ribbon. To trim bell fronts, follow pattern to stitch a piece of lace trim and a piece of ribbon to 2 bell pieces.

Pin batting to wrong side of each bell front. With right sides of bell front and back facing, stitch, leaving 2" opening. Trim batting from seam. Clip curves and turn through opening. Slipstitch closed. Following photo, tack bells to stocking.

From pink picot ribbon, cut 4 (20") and 2 (42") lengths. Fold one 42" length into 2 (5"-wide) loops. Place center of one 20" length behind loops. Tie second 20" length around center of loops and ribbons to make a bow. Repeat. Tack bows to front of stocking, using photo as guide.

BELL TREE SKIRT

Materials:
pattern and diagram on page 140
8 yards (45"-wide) green print fabric
½ yard (45"-wide) cream-on-cream print
 fabric
thread to match
3½ yards (45"-wide) thin quilt batting
4⅛ yards (½"-wide) cream
 satin ribbon
4⅛ yards (⅛"-wide) pink satin ribbon
1¾ yards (¹⁄₁₆"-wide) pink satin ribbon
2½ yards (1"-wide) cream flat
 lace trim
16 yards (¼"-wide) pink picot-edged
 ribbon
3" (½"-wide) cream Velcro
water-soluble fabric marker

Note: Add ½" seam allowance to bell pattern pieces. All seams are ½".

From green print fabric, cut 4 (60") lengths. With right sides of 2 lengths facing, align 60" edges and stitch. Repeat. Following Diagram, fold each pieced unit along seam and then in half again, forming 4 equal quarters, and pin through all layers.

From the folded corner, draw 3" and 30" arcs. (See Diagram.) Cut on arc lines through all layers. Remove stitching along one seam to form center back opening of skirt. Repeat with other pieced unit.

From green print, cut 5"-wide bias strips, piecing as needed, to make 13 yards for ruffle. Fold in half, with long edges aligned and wrong sides facing, and press. Sew a row of gathering stitches along raw edges. Divide ruffle into 8 equal sections and mark with water-soluble marker.

Cut batting into 2 (60") lengths; slipstitch pieces together along 60" edges. Cut piece to fit skirt.

Cut 28 bells from cream fabric and 14 from batting. Cut lace trim into 14 (6") lengths and ¹⁄₁₆"-wide ribbon into 14 (4½") lengths. Follow pattern to stitch lace and ribbon to 14 bells to make bell fronts.

Pin batting to wrong side of bell front. With right sides of bell front and back facing, stitch, leaving 2" opening. Trim batting from seam. Clip curves and turn through opening. Slipstitch closed. Repeat to make all 14 bells.

Using fabric marker, divide one tree skirt piece into 8 sections (sections will be 23½" wide at outer edge). Gather and pin ruffle to right side of skirt at outer edge, aligning raw edges and section marks; stitch.

Stack tree skirt pieces with right sides facing and raw edges aligned, ruffle between (with raw edges aligned), and batting on top. Stitch, beginning at one center back edge. Continue around bottom edge, up second center back edge, and around top edge, leaving opening for turning. Trim batting from seam and clip corners. Turn through opening and slipstitch closed.

Cut Velcro into 3 pieces and stitch at equal intervals down center back.

Cut cream ribbon into 7 (21") lengths. Fold ends under ½" and stitch to skirt at section marks, beginning at inner circle of skirt. (Ribbon will not go to bottom of skirt or on back opening.) Repeat with ⅛" pink ribbon, centering on cream ribbon. Machine-tack one bell at end of stitched ribbon and another 1½" above. Repeat for other bells.

From pink picot-edged ribbon, cut 14 (20") lengths and 7 (42") lengths. Fold 42" length into 2 (5") loops. Place center of one 20" length behind loops. Tie second 20" length around center of loops and ribbons to make bow. Repeat and tack bows to tops of bells.

A Glistening Garland Unfolds from Paper

A beautiful garland can add a graceful touch to any yuletide setting. Construct this radiant candle design with a pair of scissors, a paper hole punch, craft glue or cellophane tape, and decorative paper. This is a wonderful project, too, for enlisting the help of your little ones. They'll enjoy making their own garlands with blunt-tipped scissors and festive gift wrap. Follow the pattern on page 142 and soon a glowing addition to your holiday decorations will unfold.

Cut a 14″ x 2½″ strip of paper. Fan-fold the paper back and forth so that the folds fall on the dotted lines of pattern. Lightly trace pattern onto folded paper and cut out along solid lines. (*Do not cut on broken lines.*) Use a paper punch to cut out the circles on candlestick.

Connect strips with craft glue or cellophane tape. Continue until garland is desired length. Trim to wrap candles or candle holders.

Fashion Takes a Cue from the Season

Christmas attire is just the thing to get everyone in the mood for the holidays. This knitted sweater with its wraparound tree and colorful packages is a natural for those informal get-togethers during the Christmas season.

Using scrap fabrics to deck a plain sweatshirt with Christmas lights is an easy way to brighten your casual wardrobe. And to complete the look, turn Christmas minilights into fun earrings in a twinkling.

It's such a clever way to recycle burned-out lights, you might end up with a set that includes a necklace and pin to go with your earrings. Variety and craft stores carry pin backs, and to make a necklace, you can glue the lights to gold cord and add tiny gold bows where the lights and cord meet. And if you plan to give them as gifts, it will be easy to include all the ladies on your list. You might want to make it an early present, though, so that the recipients will have plenty of opportunities for modeling their festive accessories throughout the season.

One thing's for certain—whether you make them for yourself or for gifts, these seasonal fashions will quickly spread the glow of holiday cheer.

CHRISTMAS LIGHTS EARRINGS

Materials:
2 red Christmas minilight bulbs
needlenose pliers
⅛ yard (⅛"-wide) gold metallic ribbon
pair of ear posts
hot-glue gun and glue sticks

Using pliers, twist exposed filaments of light bulb at base of socket together and tuck inside socket opening. Cut ribbon in half and tie 2 bows. Glue bulb to earring backing; glue bow to socket front. Repeat for other earring. Allow glue to dry overnight.

CHRISTMAS TREE SWEATER

Materials:
charts on page 143
knitting worsted wool (100-gram skeins): 5 skeins red, 3 skeins green
small amounts of various colors of yarn for packages
sizes 5 and 7 knitting needles (or size to obtain gauge)
size 5 circular knitting needle
bobbins (optional)
stitch holder
tapestry needle
small amounts of ribbon and embroidery floss to decorate packages

SIZES: Directions are for small size (finished bust 38", finished length 22"). Changes for medium size (finished bust 40", finished length 23") and for large size (finished bust 42", finished length 24") are indicated in parentheses.

GAUGE: 5 sts and 6 rows = 1" in St st on larger needles.

Note: Since it is best not to carry thread over more than 2 sts, it may be easier to wind yarn on bobbins while working the chart. When changing colors, remember to wrap old yarn over new so that no holes occur. Be sure yarns used for packages can be cleaned in the same way as yarn for sweater.

FRONT: With smaller needles and red yarn, cast on 91 (95, 99) sts. Work in p 1, k 1 ribbing for 3". Change to larger needles, inc 4 (5, 6) sts evenly spaced across row, and beg working chart in St st. Be sure to follow chart for the appropriate size. When piece measures 19¼" (20¼", 21¼"), beg shaping neckline. Both shoulders are worked at the same time, using separate yarn. Work across 37 (39, 41) sts, slip center 21 (22, 23) sts to a stitch holder, attach new yarn and work across remaining 37 (39, 41) sts. Continue working in St st and following chart, dec 1 st

each side of neck edge every other row, 5 times. Work even until chart is completed. Bind off all sts loosely.

BACK: Cast on sts and work ribbing as for front. When ribbing is completed, change to larger needles, inc 4 (5, 6) sts evenly spaced across row, and beg working mirror image of chart in St st. Do not work dec to shape neckline. When chart is completed, piece should measure 22″ (23″, 24″). Bind off all sts loosely.

SLEEVES: With smaller needles and red, cast on 41 (43, 45) sts. Work in p 1, k 1 ribbing for 3″. Change to larger needles, inc 8 (8, 9) sts evenly spaced across row, and beg working the chart for left sleeve. When the sleeve

measures 4″, inc 1 st each edge of sleeve every ½″, 22 (22, 23) times. When sleeve measures 16¼″ (16½″, 17″) from beg, bind off all sts loosely. Work the right sleeve in the same manner except change to green after ribbing and do not work chart.

COLLAR: With larger needles and red, cast on 89 (91, 91) sts. Change to smaller needles and work in k 1, p 1 ribbing for 4″. Bind off very loosely in rib pat.

FINISHING: Using tapestry needle and matching yarn, weave shoulder seams. With red and circular needle, pick up 76 (76, 78) sts around neck. Work in k 1, p 1 ribbing for ¾″. Bind off loosely in rib pat. Measure down side seams from shoulder 9¼″ (9½″,

10″) and mark this point on front and back of sweater. Match center top of sleeve to shoulder seam and pin. Weave sleeve to sweater from point marked on front to point marked on back. Weave sleeve seam from wrist to underarm. Weave side seam from waist to underarm. Sew collar inside neck at base of ribbing. Decorate packages with ribbon and embroidery floss as desired. To attach ribbons to sweater, tack ends securely to the inside of the sweater, being careful not to split the yarn. (*Note:* Be sure to choose ribbons and floss that can be cleaned in the same way as the sweater. If the sweater is washable, preshrink the ribbons and floss before attaching to sweater.)

CHRISTMAS LIGHTS SWEATSHIRT

Materials:
patterns on page 142
white sweatshirt
⅛ yard red polished cotton
⅛ yard green polished cotton
thread to match
⅛ yard tricot-backed gold lamé fabric
¼ yard lightweight iron-on interfacing
⅛ yard double-sided fusible web
water-soluble fabric marker
2 yards (⅛″-wide) gold metallic ribbon
1 spool gold metallic thread

Note: Launder sweatshirt and polished cotton, separately, before beginning.

Apply interfacing to wrong side of red and green cotton. Transfer patterns to fabrics and cut out. Cut 10 (2″ x 3½″) pieces of fusible web. Position pieces of web and then light bulbs on sweatshirt, using photograph as guide. Trim web to fit bulbs; fuse in place. Machine-appliqué the pieces, using thread to match. Place web and then sockets and plug on sweatshirt; trim web to fit and fuse. With fabric marker, draw line for light cord; pin gold ribbon over line.

Machine-appliqué sockets and plug, using metallic thread and catching ribbon in stitching. Blindstitch ribbon in place.

Standard Knitting Abbreviations
st(s)—stitch(es)
St st—stockinette stitch (k 1 row, p 1 row)
k—knit
p—purl
inc—increase(s) (d) (ing)
beg—begin(ning)
dec—decrease(s) (d) (ing)
pat—pattern

A Notebook for Christmas Memories

Baby's first Christmas, the new bike, the year the family reunited after the children left the nest. . . . The texture of families shows in their celebrations over the years. Create a beautiful place to document those cherished events, where they'll always be at your fingertips anytime you want to enjoy the memories.

This notebook combines an old-fashioned scene, cross-stitched in subdued tones and bound with a delicate print, with the modern practicality of a purchased 3-ring binder. Stitch this holder of heirlooms and begin recording your special moments this year, or make the album for loved ones just beginning traditions of their own.

Your local office supply store or variety store will have all the materials you'll need to organize the material the notebook will hold. Try using pens with colored ink to write the category names on divider cards. You might want to include photo sections, gift lists, size charts, and Christmas card lists with a sample of your card attached and sleeves to hold cards you've received.

Punch holes in calendar pages, where you can jot down notes about parties, travel dates, and other activities. In a food category, keep track of menus you prepared (and how well they went over!), and stow away favorite recipes that you bring out only during the holidays. You might want a section just for your decorations, where you write down how you made that elegant wreath and which pieces of your family silver you used in your buffet arrangement.

This is just a sampling of the kinds of Christmas memories you can record in this notebook. But it's the kind of collection that can become a family treasure to be passed along through the years.

Materials:
chart and color key on page 141
10″ x 11½″ (3-ring) binder with 1½″ spine
14″ x 25″ piece (14-count) Rustico cloth
embroidery floss (see color key)
⅔ yard (45″-wide) cream pindot fabric for lining and sleeves
⅜″ yard (45″-wide) cream print fabric for piping
thread to match
2 yards small cording
⅜ yard batting

Note: If substituting other cross-stitch fabrics, use another 14-count for comparable results.

Make pattern from open binder and transfer it to Rustico, adding approximately 2″ all around. Mark binder panels and spine on fabric, and center cross-stitch design on right-hand panel, which will be front cover of binder. Work cross-stitch design according to chart. Trim excess fabric from binder cover to leave a ½″ seam allowance.

Transfer pattern to batting and pindot lining fabric, add ½″ seam allowance, and cut out. For inside sleeve panels, measure front of binder to spine fold, and double the width. Add ¼″ seam allowance all around, transfer twice to cream pindot fabric, and cut out 2 sleeve panels. Fold in half, wrong sides facing and short ends together.

Cut 1½″-wide bias strips from cream print fabric, piecing as needed, to make 2 yards of piping. Cover cording. With right sides facing and raw edges aligned, baste piping all around edges of Rustico. Where piping joins, peel back fabric and cut cording to just meet. Turn raw edges of this fabric to inside and whipstitch ends together.

Layer pieces as follows: Rustico design piece right side up, folded sleeve panels with raw edges to outside, lining fabric right side down, and batting. Stitch with a ½″ seam, leaving an opening to turn. Trim excess batting from seams and clip fabric at corners. Turn between sleeve panels and design piece, and whipstitch opening closed. Slip over binder.

The First Christmas in Silhouette

Flickering candlelight illuminates this cut-paper Nativity from behind, casting a reverent glow befitting the season.

The subtle cream-on-white silhouette is simple to cut. Floated between sheets of glass, it can be displayed in this standing frame, which allows you to backlight your handiwork on a table, a mantel, or in windows. Or you can place it in a purchased frame if there's no woodworker in your house.

CUT-PAPER NATIVITY

Materials:
patterns on page 144
12" x 14" piece of soft textured cream paper
12" x 14½" piece of white rice paper
craft knife
metal ruler
glue stick (optional)
2 (12⅝" x 14½") pieces of single-strength glass
silicone glue

Transfer Nativity to cream paper as indicated on pattern and cut out. Cut straight lines with the metal ruler and craft knife; cut remainder of design with scissors. Making sure all edges are flat, press finished cutting under a heavy object for several days.

Position rice paper on one piece of glass, centering it vertically. Place cutting on the rice paper. Use a tiny amount of glue stick, if necessary, to hold cutting in place.

Apply a thin line of silicone glue to the edges of glass above and below rice paper. (Keep line of glue at edge of glass so that it won't show when glass is placed in frame.) Lay second piece of glass over cutting. Place picture/glass assemblage on a firm, flat surface and weight overnight to secure bond.

FRAME

Materials:
patterns and diagram on page 144
9" x 19" (¾"-thick) piece of walnut
2¾" x 17" (¼"-thick) piece of walnut
band saw or jigsaw
electric sander
table saw or router
wood glue
#16 (1½") wire brads
penetrating oil finish

Cut ¾" walnut into the following sizes and mark with corresponding letters: (A) 2½" x 14½" for top, (B) 1¼" x 14½" for bottom support, and (C) 4½" x 19" for base. The ¼"-thick walnut (D) is part of the base.

Transfer pattern for frame top to A and cut out with a band saw. Sand or rout top edge to round it. Transfer rounded corner pattern for frame bottom to bottom support piece B. Cut out and round as above. Round edges on one side each of pieces C and D. (Rounded side is top.)

Measure thickness of picture/glass assemblage and, with a table saw or router, cut a groove that thickness and ½" deep along the bottom edge of frame top A and along the top edge of support piece B. (See Diagram.)

Apply glue to underside of piece D and center over C. Press together. Apply glue to underside of piece B, center over boards C/D and press in place. Further secure by nailing wire brads through bottom of piece D into all 3 boards.

When completely dry, sand all surfaces. Apply a penetrating oil finish, according to the package directions. Slide picture/glass assemblage into grooves on wooden frame.

Gingerbread Boys Go Hand in Hand

No home is quite complete without gingerbread treats during the holidays. But hungry admirers will have to refrain from eating these little guys. Stitched in a fanciful garland, they'll dance over the bed of your little angel, ensuring a peaceful night's visit to dreamland. Or they can add cheer to a mantel or hutch in any room of the house.

If you prefer, you can adapt the assembly to make individual tree ornaments. Simply cross-stitch a heart instead of a letter and attach a loop of grosgrain ribbon to the back of the gingerbread boy's head. Whichever way you choose to show them off, *these* goodies will last all season long!

Materials:
pattern, chart, and color key on page 142
1 yard (14-count) tan Aida cloth
3″ x 6″ red Christmas-calico fabric
7½ yards ecru piping
stuffing
red, tan, ecru thread
embroidery floss
1 yard (⅜″-wide) red satin ribbon

Trace 24 gingerbread boys from pattern onto tan fabric and 2 hearts from pattern onto red calico fabric, but do not cut out. Using 2 strands of floss, work design on Aida cloth according to chart. Work one letter on each of 12 boys' tummies so that the stitched letters spell out HAPPY HOLIDAY. Cut out all 24 gingerbread boys. Baste piping around front edges of stitched boys, making sure raw edges are aligned.

With right sides facing and raw edges aligned, pin cross-stitched boys to plain boys. Stitch together on stitching line of piping, leaving opening for turning. Clip curves and turn. Press. Stuff lightly; then blindstitch closed.

Cut out and pin hearts, right sides facing. Stitch a ¼″ seam around edge, leaving an opening for turning. Turn, stuff, and blindstitch closed.

Place boys and heart in a row so that the letters spell HAPPY HOLIDAY and the heart is between the words. Tack together as in photo. Cut ribbon in half. To hang, tack one piece of ribbon to the outside hand of each end gingerbread boy.

Stitched Tidings to Hang

The art of fine stitchery embraces the spirit of the season in this exquisite wall hanging. Its design allows the skilled needleworker to display talents in cross-stitch, piecework, appliqué, and quilting.

Hearts, flowers, trees, and seraphim cluster around the word *peace*, which is stitched in a medieval-looking script. The hanging's stylish, muted tones will blend with any decor.

Materials:
chart, color key, patterns, and diagram
   on page 146
18" x 11" (18-count) piece of
   off-white Aida cloth
embroidery floss (see color key)
⅔ yard off-white fabric
⅝ yard dark green miniprint fabric
⅓ yard red miniprint
scraps of medium and dark blue
   miniprint
19" x 37" piece of batting
19" x 37" piece of fabric for backing
½ yard (⅜"-wide) ribbon for hangers
36" curtain rod for hanging

Note: 100% cotton fabric is recommended. All seam allowances are ¼".

Work cross-stitch design according to chart. Trim to 12½" x 5½" (includes seam allowances).

From off-white, cut and label 2 (5½") squares (C); 2 (2½" x 10½") strips and 2 (2½" x 28½") strips (E). From green miniprint, cut and label 2 (1" x 5½") strips (B); 2 (1" x 6½") strips and 2 (1" x 24½") strips (D); 2 (2½" x 17½") strips and 2 (2½" x 35½") strips (H). From red miniprint, cut and label 2 (1" x 13½") strips and 2 (1" x 31½") strips (G).

Transfer appliqué and triangle pieces to fabrics indicated and cut out.

With right sides facing, sew a 5½" edge of strip B to a 5½" edge of cross-stitch piece A. Repeat for opposite edge of piece A. Trim edges and press. With right sides facing, sew a 5½" edge of piece C to 5½" edge of strip B. Repeat for opposite edge of A. (See Diagram.)

To form borders, with right sides facing, sew a 24½" edge of strip D to a long edge of pieced unit. Continue attaching D strips to remaining edges of pieced unit; miter corners and trim edges. Sew edges of strips E, right sides facing, to raw edges of strips D, mitering the corners.

Appliqué flowers and leaves to pieces C, using Diagram for placement.

To make a sawtooth border design F, sew triangles in the following order, right sides facing: off-white, green, off-white, red. Repeat design to form top and bottom border of quilt (56 triangles each) and side borders (24 triangles each, which includes corner triangles). Refer to Diagram for triangle placement at centers of top, bottom, and side borders. With right sides facing, sew these pieced strips F to raw edges of quilt pieces E. With right sides facing, sew strips G to raw edges of F, mitering the corners. Attach H to G in same way.

Stack pieces in the following order: backing fabric (right side down), batting, and pieced top (right side up). Outline-quilt appliquéd pieces. Transfer heart pattern to border E and quilt. Quilt-in-the-ditch around all border seams.

For hangers, cut ribbon into 7 (2") pieces, fold each in half, and attach to top of wall hanging, aligning raw edges and referring to Diagram for placement.

Evenly trim all edges and turn under backing and top piece edges ¼". Blindstitch all around. Slide rod through loops.

Mrs. Rudolph's Sewing Box

Here's an endearing creature to make from your scrap bag. Details make this darling reindeer look intricate, but she's actually fairly simple to make. The box she tops can house a gift and then serve as a sewing caddy, candy box, or Christmas keepsake.

Materials:
patterns on page 148
⅛ yard (36"-wide) tan fleece
⅛ yard (36"-wide) red-and-green miniprint
  fabric
red pindot fabric scraps
green ministripe fabric scraps
thread: red, green, and black
stuffing
2 (⅛") round black buttons for eyes
¼" red pom-pom for nose
hot-glue gun and glue sticks
pink colored pencil
embroidery floss: red, green
2 yards (½"-wide) flat white
  lace trim
2 small twigs for antlers
4" (⅛"-wide) red polka-dot satin ribbon
6" (⅜"-wide) red-and-green
  striped ribbon
¼" brass jingle bell
novelty toys to fill stocking
green spray paint
4" wooden heart box
miniature wooden spool
  of thread
brass sewing needle

Note: Add ⅛" seam allowance to all pattern pieces.

Transfer patterns to fabric and cut out. With right sides facing, stitch fleece and pindot ear pieces together, leaving open where indicated on pattern. Turn, slipstitch closed, and gather where indicated.

With right sides facing, stitch head/body pieces together, leaving open where indicated on pattern. Turn, stuff, and slipstitch closed. Repeat for arms and legs. Following pattern, tack arms, legs, and ears to head/body. Sew eyes to face. To make eyelashes, with doubled black thread, stitch back and forth through head 6 times, leaving loops on each side. Cut loops and trim. Glue on red pom-pom nose and lightly shade cheeks with pink colored pencil. Following photo, embroider red mouth.

Cut a 1¾"-diameter circle from red-and-green miniprint for cap. Fold cap edge under ⅛" and attach lace trim, using small gathering stitches. Gather, lightly stuff cap, and glue to head, behind ears. Tie polka-dot ribbon in bow and tack between ears. With scissors, make snips in head below ears for antlers. Place glue on ends of twigs for antlers and insert at an angle.

Stitch side/underarm seams of dress, right sides facing. Cut pieces of trim to fit bottom of dress and sleeve ends. Turn under ⅛" hem at bottom of dress and sleeves and stitch, attaching trim. Stitch shoulder seams, right sides facing, using pattern as a guide. Turn dress right side out and press. Turn under neck edge. Attach trim around neck edge on right side, using small gathering stitches.

Put dress on reindeer and gather to fit neck; knot securely. Tie a bow with red-and-green striped ribbon and tack to dress under chin. Glue jingle bell below bow.

Stitch stocking, right sides facing, along sides and bottom. Turn and press. Fold top of stocking to inside and stitch. Cut and glue trim to front of stocking and red pindot heart to heel. (See photo.) Lightly stuff stocking, inserting novelty toys and securing with glue. With red embroidery floss, make small loop for hanging.

Paint heart box and lid; allow to dry. Glue trim around rim of box lid at top. Glue reindeer to top of lid. (See photo.) Wrap wooden spool with green embroidery floss and glue ends. Glue spool and stocking in place. (See photo.) Slip needle into hand.

A Flock of Feathered Ornaments

One partridge in a pear tree is simply not enough when you see this flock of feathered fellows. A cross-stitched cardinal with a brightly colored scarf is quickly stitched and framed. Deep colors and velvet piping give an embroidered quail elegance, and golden geese add a new reflection when decorating a tree or wreath.

GOLDEN GEESE ORNAMENTS

Materials (for 1 goose):
patterns on page 149
4″ square (36-gauge) tooling brass
dry ballpoint pen or pointed instrument
scraps (36-gauge) tooling copper and
    aluminum
craft glue
hot-glue gun and glue sticks
4″ scrap of ribbon (optional)

Tape paper patterns to metal, place metal on soft surface (small piece of felt works well), and transfer patterns with a dry ballpoint pen or other pointed instrument. Cut out pieces with scissors. On firm surface, smooth cut edges with the bowl of a spoon.

Working with the dry ballpoint pen and placing the metal on felt, transfer details as follows. From the front of pieces: outline of eye and beak line. From the back of pieces: wing feathers, bowknot and its puckers, pupil of eye, and eyelashes.

Follow photo and patterns and use craft glue to attach pieces in the following order: feet to back of body, wings and beak to front, and bow to front. If any pieces need slight adjustment, trim with scissors. Use hot-glue gun to attach goose to wreath or to attach a ribbon hanger to back, if desired.

CROSS-STITCH CARDINAL

Materials:
chart and color key on page 149
5″ square (14-count) white Aida cloth
embroidery floss (see color key)
red seed beads
pale pink seed beads
3¼″ circular cross-stitch frame
5″ square of batting
craft glue (optional)

Stitch design according to chart. To finish, place design in frame with batting behind it and trim to fit.

If desired, wrap frame with embroidery floss, securing thread with dots of glue. To make hanger, loop a 7″ length of floss through back of ornament and tie in a knot.

EMBROIDERED QUAIL ORNAMENT

Materials:
chart, color key, and pattern on page 149
6″ square even-weave fabric
#8 tapestry needle
embroidery floss (see color key)
6″ x 12″ piece of cardboard
6″ square of batting
14″ square green velveteen
thread to match
½ yard (¼″) cording
7″ piece of metallic cord

Trace embroidery design onto even-weave fabric and work, according to chart, using 2 strands of floss. Using heart pattern, cut 2 from cardboard, one from batting, and one from velveteen. Adding ½″ all around, center heart pattern over design and cut out. Run a gathering stitch all along edge. Sandwich batting between fabric and cardboard back. Gather fabric snugly against cardboard and tie off.

From velveteen, cut 14″ x 1¼″ bias strip and, with cording, make piping. With raw edges aligned, hand-stitch piping to heart,

beginning and ending at top of heart. Fold a 3″ x ¾″ piece of velveteen in half lengthwise, roll into rosebud, and tack to top of heart. For backing, turn under raw edges of velveteen heart. Turn raw edges of piping to back of heart. Hand-stitch backing to piping. Make a loop with gold cord for hanger.

75

Patchwork Peppermint Duo

Brightly striped peppermint candy is the inspiration for this graphic stocking and wreath.

A bit of clever piecework results in bold stripes zigzagging around the plump stuffed wreath. On the ample stocking, striped squares take on a checkerboard pattern, and a layer of batting cushions the load of goodies. Finished with Christmas green, the set trumpets the traditional colors of the season in a modern, playful key.

PEPPERMINT WREATH

Materials:
patterns and diagram on page 150
½ yard (36"-wide) green fabric
½ yard (36"-wide) red-and-white striped fabric
½ yard batting
stuffing
2½ yards (¼"-wide) red bias tape
thread to match

Note: Add ¼" seam allowance to all pattern pieces.

Transfer patterns and markings and cut the following: From green fabric, cut 12 pieces of pattern A; reverse pattern and cut 12 more. Also from green, cut 12 pieces of pattern C; reverse, cut 12. From red-and-white striped fabric, cut 2 (2⅜" x 36") strips for bow. From remaining red-and-white striped fabric, cut 12 pieces from pattern B, and 12 reversed, aligning fabric stripes with pattern arrows.

Referring to Diagram, stitch piece A to B, and then to C. Repeat for reverse pieces. Stitch these pieced sections together to make wreath unit; press seams open. Repeat

these steps to create 11 more wreath units. Stitch all units together, forming ring. Press seams.

Using wreath as a pattern, cut 2 from batting and one from green fabric for backing. Stack in the following order: backing (right side down), 2 layers batting, wreath front (right side up). Pin inner and outer circle edges, baste. Zigzag ¼" from edges of inner and outer circles, leaving 3 (3") openings evenly spaced around outside of wreath. Trim all layers.

Add stuffing between batting layers; whipstitch openings closed. Whipstitch bias tape all around inner and outer wreath edges.

To make bow, stitch long edges together, right sides facing. Turn and press. Turn edges of ends in, whipstitch closed. Tie bow; tack 5" piece of bias tape to back of bow; then use to attach bow to wreath.

PEPPERMINT STOCKING

Materials:
patterns and diagram on page 150
½ yard (36"-wide) red-and-white striped fabric
¼ yard (36"-wide) green fabric
½ yard (36"-wide) fabric for backing
¾ yard (36"-wide) fabric for lining
¾ yard batting
thread to match
2 yards (¼"-wide) green bias tape

Note: Add ¼" seam allowance to all pattern pieces.

Transfer patterns and markings to fabrics and cut out. Using Diagram, arrange fabric pieces for assembly so that stripes follow direction of arrows. With right sides facing, sew into rows. Stitch rows together. Stitch other striped pieces onto striped rows.

To attach remaining pattern pieces to stocking, with right sides facing, stitch cuff and then toe. Stitch straight sides of heel. Press seams.

Using pieced stocking front as a pattern, cut one stocking back, 2 of batting, and 2 of lining. (Reverse pattern for one lining piece.) To make stocking back, stack pieces in the following order: back (right side down), batting, and lining (right side up). Align edges, baste, and trim. To make stocking front, stack lining (right side down), batting, and pieced stocking front (right side up). Baste front and back together and trim edges.

To finish top edge of stocking front, zigzag ¼" from edge and trim. Bind stitched edge with bias tape. Repeat to finish top edge of stocking back.

Stitch stocking back and front together, linings facing, using ¼" seam and leaving top open. Zigzag edges, trim and bind with bias tape, leaving 4" piece of tape at top back for hanger. Turn under raw edges of tape and stitch. Loop and tack to stocking.

Wrap Your Gift in Keepsake Stitchery

Traditional tokens of Christmas spices and spirits can be personalized with easy-to-construct bags, adorned with Christmas cross-stitch. Christmas lists grow short when wonderful wraps are whipped up by the dozens and then filled with carefully chosen bottles and fragrant spices. After what hides inside is enjoyed, the clever bags go on to make handsome additions to Christmas decor for years to come.

SANTA BOTTLE BAG

Materials:
chart, color key, and diagram
   on page 148
13″ x 14½″ (28-count) piece of charcoal
   Jobelan
#24 tapestry needle
embroidery floss (see color key)
thread to match Jobelan
18″ piece of gold braid

Center design 6½″ from sides and 7¼″ from top of fabric, working design according to the chart. Use 2 strands of floss for cross-stitch, working over 2 threads, and one for backstitch. Use 2 strands of gray floss for eyebrows and to outline mustache and beard; use 2 strands of black floss for lettering and to outline details in robe. Block.

With right sides facing, stitch 13″ edges together, using ½″ seam; press seam open. Press top edge under ¼″ twice to inside and stitch. Press bag flat with design centered in front and seam in back. With right sides facing, stitch bottom edges together, using ½″ seam. Stitch corners of bag bottom (see Diagram) and turn bag right side out. Knot braid ends and tack center of braid to back at seam about 2″ from top.

SIMMERING SPICE BAG

Materials:
chart and color key on page 149
5″ x 10″ piece of Fiddler's cloth
#24 tapestry needle
embroidery floss (see color key)
thread to match Fiddler's cloth
⅔ yard (1⁄16″-wide) red satin ribbon

Fold fabric with 5″ edges together and fold on bottom. Center design on front of one panel of fabric. Work design according to chart, using one strand of floss for backstitch and 2 strands of floss for cross-stitch. Block.

Measure 1½″ from each end and pull 4 horizontal threads (one square of fabric) for casing for ribbon. With right sides facing, stitch side edges, using ½″ seam; press seam open and turn. Fringe top edge of bag by pulling horizontal threads down to ½″. Using tapestry needle, weave ribbon through pulled-thread casing, beginning and ending above center of design. Fill bag with simmering spices, attach recipe card with ribbon, and tie ribbon in bow.

Recipe Card for Simmering Spices:

  1 **orange**
  1 **lemon**
  ¼ **cup cinnamon sticks**
  ¼ **cup whole cloves**

Slice ½ orange and ½ lemon thinly; spread to dry for several days. Add ¼ cup cinnamon stick pieces and whole cloves to the dried fruit mixture. Add water and simmer potpourri for delightful scents to spice the holidays.

Rustic Creations in Wood

Folk artist Lorraine Erwin is known for her rustically painted creations in wood. The simple bunny and heart rings shown here add whimsy to the table, but they can also be mounted on the wall to hold hand towels. Lorraine's wooden sleigh makes a striking container for greenery and candles, flower arrangements, or a small load of Santa's booty. For more on Lorraine and her holiday decorations, see page 32.

NAPKIN RINGS

These rings are simple to make from scraps of plywood. Simply transfer a heart or bunny pattern from page 153 to a 6" square of ½"-thick plywood and cut out with a band saw or jigsaw. Drill a hole in the middle for inner cutout, insert blade of saw, and cut out inner circle or heart. For the bunny, chisel or gouge details in ears, around tail, and for eye. Apply a thin coat of flat acrylic paint, letting patches of wood show through, and let dry. Paint details of bunny as shown in photo.

WOODEN SLEIGH

Materials:
patterns on page 152
1¼ feet x 3⅔ feet of ½″ plywood
band saw or jigsaw
sandpaper
wood filler
wood glue
finishing nails
red, black flat acrylic paint

Transfer patterns to plywood and cut out. With wood filler, fill any imperfections in plywood and sand all surfaces smooth. Position back and front of sleigh between side pieces, glue, and nail in place. Position this sleigh framework on bottom piece, glue, and nail in place. Referring to photo, position runners and glue and nail in place.

Refer to pattern and photo to paint sleigh. To achieve antiqued look, wipe a bit of black paint over red surface with a rag, letting texture catch color. Paint details freehand for a folk art effect, or stencil if you prefer. For small hearts on runners, sand edges a little unevenly, paint, and let dry. Glue in place on runners.

Crochet Delicate Hearts and Flowers

Turn bright red crochet thread into a filet crochet runner to grace your Christmas table and keepsake poinsettias to top your packages. The heart design of the runner is appropriate not only to the Christmas season, but to any time that friends and loved ones gather to share a meal. The package-trim holiday flowers can also be used to accent greenery on a mantel or, wired to a wreath, as a stunning door decoration.

POINSETTIA

Materials:
50-gram ball red crochet thread, size 10
#8 steel crochet hook
starch
gold bugle beads
gold metallic thread
florists' wire (optional)

POINSETTIA PETALS (make 5): Ch 6, join with a sl st to form a ring. *Row 1:* Ch 3, 5 dc in ring, turn. *Rows 2-4:* Ch 3, inc 1 st, 1 dc in each dc, inc 1 st, turn (12 dc after row 4). *Rows 5-9:* Ch 3, 1 dc in each dc across, turn. *Rows 10-13:* Sl st in first st to dec 1 st, ch 3, 1 dc in each dc, stop 1 st from edge for 2nd dec, turn (4 sts remain after row 13). *Row 14:* Sl st in first st, ch 2, 1 dc in next st, fasten off. To work remaining petals, join yarn with sl st in ring, turn, and rep rows 1-14.

FINISHING: Soak poinsettia briefly in a very diluted starch solution to stiffen slightly. Lay flat to dry. Allow flower to dry completely before attaching gold bugle beads with gold thread for centers of poinsettia (see photograph). Florists' wire can be threaded through a few stitches on the backs of the petals to curve them.

TABLE RUNNER

Materials:
chart on page 154
3 (50-gram) balls red crochet thread,
   size 10
#8 steel crochet hook
spray starch

TABLE RUNNER: *Row 1:* Ch 8, dc in first ch
to form first square of chart, turn. *Row 2:* Ch
6, 1 dc in edge st, 3 dc in sp, ch 2, sk 1 ch, 1 tr
in next ch, turn.

Continue to follow chart row by row,
working back and forth. To inc at beg of row,
ch 6, 1 dc in edge st. To inc at end of row, ch
2, 1 tr in edge st.

After top of bow (row 46) is completed, rep
row 47, 51 times (or work number of rows
required to obtain desired length). Then follow chart to complete design. To dec at beg
of row, sl st over to 2nd square of row, ch 3.
To dec at end of row, leave last square
unworked. Do not fasten off after last row of
chart.

EDGING: *Row 1:* Sc around edge of piece.
Row 2: * Ch 4, (sc in next st, ch 1) 3 times, rep
from * around. *Row 3:* * (1 dc, ch 1) 8 times in
ch-4 sp, ch 1, 1 sc in center sc, ch 1, rep from
* around. Fasten off.

FINISHING: Press and spray-starch piece.
Pin flat to dry.

Standard Crochet Abbreviations

ch—chain
dc—double crochet
st(s)—stitch(es)
sp—space
sk—skip
tr—triple crochet
inc—increase

beg—beginning
dec—decrease
sl—slip
sc—single crochet
rep—repeat
*—repeat instructions following asterisk
   as indicated

Sculpted Paper Angels

Hark! These angelic ornaments and cards will dramatically herald the season, as they float on the limbs of your tree and carry your greetings near and far.

Using ceramic cookie molds, bathroom tissue, and papier-mâché, you can quickly and inexpensively make dozens of the celestial beauties. Children will especially enjoy participating in the process, but save the final trimming for older members of the family.

For variety, use colored tissue or water tinted with food coloring. And if your mold is symmetrical, glue a couple of ornaments back-to-back, perhaps with a bit of lace between, for two-sided decorations.

Materials:
1 lb. package Celluclay instant papier-mâché, from craft shop (or make your own)
ceramic cookie molds
vegetable oil
plain white bathroom tissue
#5 paintbrush
small container of water
small container of water and white glue, in equal proportions
#8 stencil brush
sharp craft knife
2" length of crochet cotton or string
gold acrylic paint
gold metallic ink
fine artists' brush
clear acrylic spray finish
8" gold cording

Note: Read all the way through instructions before beginning. Make one ornament as a test. Don't be discouraged—it gets easier with practice, and the results get better and better!

Mix papier-mâché and set aside. Coat inside of mold with vegetable oil; wipe out excess.

Place one layer of tissue in mold. Dip #5 paintbrush in water and gently tamp paper into mold to shape it to the contours (Photo 1). Allow any excess tissue to extend beyond the rim of cookie mold.

In a similar manner, add additional layers of tissue, one at a time, to the mold, working slowly and carefully so as not to tear the paper.

Note: It will not be necessary to wet the brush again before adding the second and third layers, because the tissue will absorb all the water it needs from the layers below. Wet the brush about every fourth layer, or as needed for tissue to stick to the previous layers.

After 8 layers, switch from water to a water/glue solution for added strength. At

this point you can also switch to the stencil brush and begin working faster and tamping harder to pack tissue firmly into mold. You can even apply 2 layers at a time.

After building up about 18 layers, finish filling cavity of mold with papier-mâché, pressing firmly into place (Photo 2). Level just to rim of mold. Wipe any excess papier-mâché away from rim, leaving edges of tissue still extending beyond rim.

Now add 8 more layers of tissue, using plain water, to cover the papier-mâché.

To remove the ornament, invert mold and rap back several times with the back of a wooden spoon. Then turn over and pull ragged edges of tissue gently. (Bits of paper may stick to mold in places. To repair ornament, simply wet the #5 paintbrush with plain water and tap torn edges gently in place.) Place ornament face up on wax paper and let dry overnight. When dry to touch, turn ornament over and let dry 24 hours or more, until completely dry.

With a sharp craft knife, trim away any excess tissue, using a gentle sawing motion (Photo 3).

To add hanger, fold cotton string in half to make loop, lay ends on top back of ornament, and dab with white glue to hold in place. Then add 2 or 3 small pieces of wet tissue over ends of string to reinforce. Let glue and tissue dry.

Using fine artists' brush, highlight selected details with gold acrylic paint. Let dry. Then apply second coat with gold metallic ink to add shimmer. Let details dry thoroughly.

Spray lightly with clear acrylic finish to protect ornament. Let dry.

Tie cording to loop for hanger.

To make cards, prepare angel ornament and allow to dry as instructed above. Fold a piece of heavy blotter or craft paper in half to form a card. To glue angel ornament to front of card, wet card slightly with glue and water solution and add 1 or 2 layers of tissue, gently tapping tissue around edges of angel to secure. To prevent curling, pin edges of card down while it dries.

Wildlife Stitchery for the Outdoorsman

A bit of waste canvas, a few minutes spent cross-stitching, and voila! That purchased gift for the outdoorsman on your list becomes a one-of-a-kind creation. Use the charts and color keys on page 154 to embellish a scarf and shirt, as shown here. Or stitch one of these creatures of the wild on a stadium blanket, fabric toiletries bag, or hunting vest.

This deer and mallard were stitched with 2 strands of floss on 14-count waste canvas, but you can vary the count to fit the item your stitchery will adorn. Just baste the canvas in place and stitch the design according to the chart. Then, remove the basting stitches, wet the canvas, and carefully pull out the waste canvas threads, one by one. If needed, block item as it dries.

Personal Style: Details that Count

From festive accessories, to distinctive package toppers and cards, to the present you give your favorite little Christmas cherub, personal style is what sets you apart. And this style needn't take hours to create. Most of the items shown here are as quick in the making as they are attractive, leaving time to leisurely enjoy the season.

Dressing for the holidays includes a festive hair ornament for each of the ladies of the house. Elegant fabric, shiny ribbon, dried flowers, and jewels lend themselves to the subject at hand. Turn these scraps and baubles into enviable accessories with a hot-glue gun and barrettes or hairbands.

For gift tags and cards, bits of lace become stencils and stamped details finish the effect. And your costume jewelry, seashells, and other trinkets make gift boxes handsome enough to outlast the season.

BABY REINDEER

Materials:
patterns on page 151
1 yard (45″-wide) white fleece
¼ yard (45″-wide) brown fleece
thread to match
2″ square red felt
16-ounce bag stuffing
2 (1″) round black-and-white shank
    buttons (for younger children, eyes may
    be embroidered)
1″ red pom-pom
hot-glue gun and glue sticks
powder blusher

Note: Add ½″ seam allowance to all pattern pieces.

Transfer patterns to fabric and cut out. Cut one 14″ x 20″ piece of white fleece for body, one 3½″ x 10″ piece for neck, and 4 (8″) squares for legs. From brown fleece, cut 2 (5″ x 9″) pieces for antlers and 4 (4″) squares for antler points.

With right sides facing and raw edges aligned, stitch short edges of body piece together to form cylinder. Run a line of gathering stitches ½″ from edge on each end of cylinder; pull to gather one end and knot securely. Turn and stuff tightly. Pull gathers on other end, tucking raw edges in. Knot securely. Repeat for legs, neck, and head. To assemble, slipstitch legs to bottom (seam side) of cylinder, about 1″ from seam. On opposite (top) side of cylinder, stitch neck at one end, with seam facing front. Attach head to neck, seam side down, placing larger end on neck.

To make antler, fold in half, right sides facing, with 9″ sides together. To shape, begin tapering seam at 5″ so that end of antler is 1″ across. Trim excess fabric. Run a line of gathering stitches ½″ from each end and pull to gather on small end first; then stuff and finish as above. Repeat for other antler.

To make antler points, repeat cylinder process with each 4″ square, tapering one end to 1″ width; finish as directed. Repeat for remaining small points.

To form curve in antler, run a line of gathering stitches along side opposite seam; pull to gather fabric slightly, forming curve. Knot securely. Repeat for other antler and antler points. Position and stitch 2 antler points to each large antler. To attach antler to head, position and stitch to back of head, antlers pointed in. (See photo.)

To make ear, repeat cylinder process, placing straight sides together. Do not stuff. Repeat for other ear. At base of antlers, stitch large ends of ears to head and to seams of antlers.

Make tail like ear, using brown fleece. Position and attach large end of tail at top rear of body.

To shape face, run a line of gathering stitches around muzzle, 3″ from front of head. Pull to desired fullness and knot. Glue straight edge of tongue inside gathers on end of muzzle. For eyes, sew buttons just above gathered line defining muzzle. For nose, glue pom-pom 2″ above mouth.

Lightly dust insides of ears and cheeks with powder blusher. Tie bow or scarf around neck as desired.

CHILD'S ROSEBUD BARRETTE

Beginning with the tiniest subject, a small, brass-plated barrette is decorated with dried flowers and secures a young lady's curls. To make, glue dried fern and then rosebuds to cover barrette. Add two bows of 1/16″ ribbon and seed pearls to complete.

TAPESTRY BOW

Making a flat bow for the back of the head requires a piece of tapestry fabric, approximately 16″ square, and a hair clasp. To make bow, cut a 14″ square. Fold 2 opposite sides to center, and then remaining 2 sides, and glue. Pinch at center and secure by wrapping with thread. Cut 2″ x 4″ piece from remaining fabric. Fold 4″ edges to center. Wrap this strip around center of bow, gluing to secure. Glue completed bow to bar of barrette.

BERIBBONED HAIRBAND

Cut 34″ piece of ribbon; angle one end. Beginning with angled end of ribbon, glue and wrap ribbon around head band, diagonally, keeping ribbon tight and smooth. Securely glue ends, covering band and folding ends under.

To make bow, use 47″ of ribbon to form 6 loops, securing at center with thread or wire. Use the remaining 9″ piece of ribbon to tie bow to band; cut V-notches in ends of ribbon. Decorate bow by gluing hemlock cones, canella berries, and balsam to center.

STENCILED CARDS AND GIFT TAGS

Arrange scraps of lace as stencils on pieces of card-stock weight paper and spray with acrylic paint. Let dry.

To make rubber stamp, trace a design onto flat rubber eraser, remembering that design will be reversed. Cut ⅛″ deep around design. Use ink pad, acrylic paint, or felt-tip pen to paint design on stamp for printing on card. Make holes for ribbon as desired.

EMBELLISHED GIFT BOXES

Wrap bottom of box with gift paper. Wrap lid of box and then decorate with ribbons. Glue gold beads, seed pearls, tiny shells, or pieces of costume jewelry to bow.

A Tree of Ribbon Loops

Simple ribbon loops, in abundance, form this Christmas Ribbon Tree. Start with a craft foam cone, spray-painting it to match your choice of ribbon. (A 12″ cone requires approximately 25-30 yards of 2″-wide ribbon.) Cut 22-gauge florists' wire into 2″-4″ pieces to secure each loop.

Using uncut ribbon, make a 2″ loop with a 3″ tail on one side. Secure loop with a piece of wire and push twisted ends of wire into the top of cone. Keep making these loops in ribbon and fastening into cone with wire,

increasing size of loops as you go toward bottom of cone. Secure at bottom, leaving streamer of ribbon, as desired, and cutting it on the diagonal. Continue this process to cover cone, beginning each row as close to top of cone as possible, until desired fullness is achieved.

Trim ribbons at top of cone on the diagonal. Tie a small piece of ribbon around these ribbons to make a feathery tip. To curl streamers, steam, then roll them in tight curls. Secure with paper clips until dry.

Craft a Country Quilt Rack

Whether your favorite quilt is a family heirloom or one that you just finished last week, it is a prized piece of handwork. And what better way to display it than on this handsome quilt rack? A challenging project that yields eye-catching results, the rack, with our detailed instructions, is easily assembled and decorated. Patterns and diagrams are provided for the stencil design shown here or, if you're daring, use the same technique and adapt a pattern of your own, to set off the beauty of your quilt.

Materials:
patterns on page 155
table saw
8 feet of pine 1 x 12
sandpaper
band saw or scroll saw
router with ⅜″-radius cornering bit
wood glue
finishing nails
wood putty
light wood stain
2 yards clear adhesive shelf paper
craft knife with sharp blade
metal ruler
dark wood-tone florists' spray paint
red florists' spray paint
paste wax

Note: Florists' spray paint is easy to use and dries quickly. However, if it is not available in your local florist's shop, regular spray paint may be used.

With table saw, cut from pine: 2 (32″ x 10″) pieces for ends, 2 (28″ x 2½″) pieces for side cross members, and 2 (26½″ x 2½″) pieces for top and bottom cross members. (See Diagram 1 for layout.) Sand all pieces smooth and mark positions.

Note: After each cut, re-measure next piece, to prevent slippage or variance.

Transfer curve details from patterns to end pieces and cut with band saw. Sand smooth.

If rounded edges are desired, round one corner of each of the 2 side cross members with router. Rout full round on one side of the top cross member. Sand all pieces smooth.

Lay the 2 end pieces on their sides. Mark the location of one side cross member on each end piece, fitting ends of side cross members into notches in end pieces. (See Diagram 2 for placement.) Glue and nail in place. Carefully turn unit over to opposite side and attach other side cross member in same manner.

Stand unit upright and mark location of the top and bottom cross members on the inside surfaces of the end pieces.

Align top and bottom cross members with location marks and attach them between the two end pieces with wood glue and nails (see Diagram 2).

Allow glue to dry thoroughly. To set nails below surface of wood, place a second nail against nail head and tap gently with a hammer. Cover nail heads with wood putty. When dry, sand all parts smooth.

Apply a light wood stain over entire rack. Allow to dry. Mark center of end pieces for design placement. Using a pencil and a metal ruler, transfer all patterns onto end pieces. (See Diagram 3.)

To mask design areas while painting rest of rack, firmly rub adhesive shelf paper over

them. Using ruler as a guide, use craft knife to trim paper along outside edges of all designs. Pull away edges from wood, making sure remaining paper adheres firmly to design areas.

Spray entire rack with dark wood-tone florists' spray paint. (Florists' paint will dry immediately. If using other type paint, allow to dry completely.) Remove adhesive shelf paper.

To add red details, cover entire surface of end pieces with another sheet of clear adhesive shelf paper. Cut adhesive paper away from design areas and peel away paper cut-outs. Leaving the rest of the surface masked, spray design areas with red paint. Strip away all adhesive shelf paper. If using paint other than florists' paint, let dry completely.

To finish, rub paste wax over stenciled designs and buff for a soft luster.

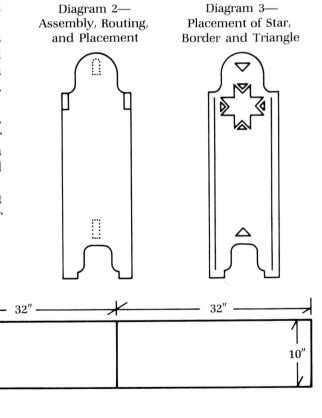

Diagram 2—
Assembly, Routing,
and Placement

Diagram 3—
Placement of Star,
Border and Triangle

Diagram 1—Cutting Layout for 1 x 12 Pine

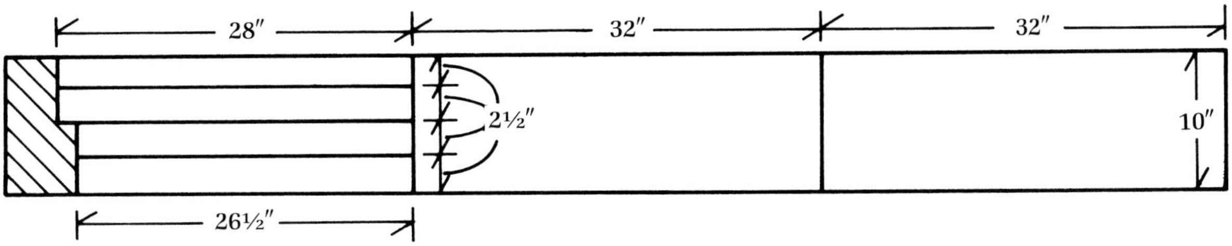

28″   32″   32″

2½″   26½″   10″

Heavenly Gift Bags

For the little angels on your list, bag gifts in these sweet receptacles for trinkets. Made from scraps of glitter and lace out of your sewing box, these happy button angels with their perky stitched smiles will continue to bring delight long after their cargo has been revealed.

Materials (for 1 bag):
patterns on page 154
¼ yard light-colored fabric
scrap of interfacing
1¼" covered-button kit
embroidery floss: brown, deep pink
thread to match fabric
lace, trim, braid, and yarn scraps
⅛" ribbon

Note: Add ½" seam allowance to bag.

Transfer patterns to fabric and interfacing and cut out. Cut circle of fabric to cover 1¼" button, using pattern in button kit.

Embroider face on fabric circle (see photo), making brown eyes with French knots and pink mouth with one feather stitch. Cover button with face, using instructions in button kit.

Stack a wing (right side down), interfacing wing, and wing (right side up) with edges aligned. Satin-stitch the 2 curved edges by machine. Using pattern for placement, stitch straight edge of wing to bag front, with tip of wing pointed toward center of bag. Fold wing back over stitching so that wing points away from center; press and stitch close to fold. Repeat to make and attach the other wing.

Fold top of bag pieces to wrong side along fold line marked on pattern; stitch ½" from folded edges.

Add trim and lace to decorate front of bag, referring to photo; stitch. With right sides facing, stitch bag along sides and bottom, beginning and ending below casings and using ½" seam. (Be careful not to catch wings in bag seams.) Clip the corners, turn, and press.

Use several 5" lengths of yarn to make hair for angel, braiding, looping, and decorating as desired. Attach hair to button face at top and sides. Make halo from trim and sew to back of button. Sew button face to bag, referring to pattern for placement. Thread ribbon through casing to close bag.

Celebrations from the Kitchen

Christmas offers more chances to eat delicious food than any other holiday, and Southerners take full advantage of that fact. For weeks ahead, treats come out a few at a time—when friends drop by, at office parties, for open houses. And as for the big meal . . . well, time seems to stop for awhile afterwards. This chapter is full of recipes for all of those occasions, from a decidedly feminine tea party to a buffet dinner that's a snap to prepare. So get out the spices. It's time to cook!

A Sugar and Spice Tea Party

When a gathering of friends includes two generations of ladies, the event takes on special charm. The dishes presented here perfectly complement a holiday tea party for moms and their daughters. From Crêpe Ham Rollups to Butter Cookies, this party includes just about everything nice.

CRÊPE HAM ROLLUPS

    1   (8-ounce) package cream cheese, softened
    3   tablespoons mayonnaise
    1   tablespoon chopped chives
    2   teaspoons lemon juice
    ½   teaspoon dried whole dillweed
    ¼   teaspoon onion powder
    ¼   teaspoon paprika
    ⅛   to ¼ teaspoon red pepper
   12   (6-inch) crêpes (recipe follows)
   12   (4-inch-square) slices boiled ham

Combine first 8 ingredients in a small mixing bowl; beat at medium speed of an electric mixer until blended.

Spread a heaping tablespoon of cream cheese mixture evenly over each crêpe; top with a ham slice. Roll each crêpe jellyroll fashion; wrap in wax paper and chill at least 1 hour. Slice into ½-inch pieces when ready to serve. Yield: 7 dozen.

Crêpes

    1   cup all-purpose flour
    ¼   teaspoon salt
   1¼   cups milk
    2   eggs
    2   tablespoons butter or margarine, melted
        Vegetable oil

Combine flour, salt, and milk, and beat at medium speed of an electric mixer until smooth. Add eggs and beat well; stir in butter. Refrigerate batter at least 2 hours. (This allows flour particles to swell and soften so that crêpes will be light in texture.)

Brush bottom of a 6-inch crêpe pan or heavy skillet lightly with oil; place over medium heat until just hot, not smoking.

Pour 2 tablespoons batter into pan; quickly tilt pan in all directions so that batter covers pan in a thin film. Cook 1 minute or until lightly browned.

Lift edge of crêpe to test for doneness. Crêpe is ready for flipping when it can be shaken loose from pan. Flip crêpe and cook about 30 seconds on other side. (This side is usually spotty brown and is the side on which filling is placed.)

Place crêpes on a towel to cool. Stack between layers of wax paper to prevent sticking. Repeat until all batter is used. Yield: 15 (6-inch) crêpes.

Opposite: A holiday tea for the ladies, both little and big, includes, from front, Spice Cookies, Cinnamon Toast Sticks, Orange Dip for fresh fruit, Pecan Cups, Children's Party Sandwiches, Chicken Salad Bites, Crêpe Ham Rollups, and Chocolate Madeleines.

Above: For these little girls, sugar and spice includes delicious Butter Cookies dipped in green and pink candy coatings. While the grown-up ladies sip freshly brewed tea, the young ones are poured commercial red punch.

CINNAMON TOAST STICKS

⅓ cup sugar
1 teaspoon ground cinnamon
1 (11-ounce) package commercial
    soft breadsticks
3 tablespoons butter or margarine,
    melted

Combine sugar and cinnamon. Set aside.
Cut breadsticks in half lengthwise. Dip each half in butter; roll in cinnamon mixture. Twist each strip 2 or 3 times and place on ungreased baking sheets. Bake at 350° for 15 to 18 minutes. Let cool on wire racks. Yield: 16 toast sticks.

ORANGE DIP

2 egg yolks
¼ cup sugar
⅛ teaspoon salt
2 tablespoons orange juice
    concentrate, thawed and
    undiluted
1 teaspoon grated orange rind
1⅓ cups whipping cream

Combine egg yolks, sugar, and salt in top of a double boiler; bring water to a boil. Reduce heat to very low; cook 8 to 10 minutes, or until mixture reaches 165°, stirring constantly. (Mixture will be very thick and light in color.) Remove from heat; stir in orange juice concentrate and rind. Cool.
Beat whipping cream until soft peaks form; fold orange mixture into whipped cream. Cover and chill at least 2 hours. Serve with fresh fruit. Yield: 2⅔ cups.

CHICKEN SALAD BITES

3 cups finely chopped cooked
    chicken
¼ cup finely chopped celery
¼ cup sweet pickle relish
¼ cup cooked salad dressing (recipe
    follows)
2 to 3 tablespoons mayonnaise
1 to 2 tablespoons minced onion
¼ teaspoon pepper
    Paprika
    Chopped fresh parsley
    Finely chopped toasted almonds

Combine first 7 ingredients; chill. Shape mixture into 1-inch balls and roll each in paprika, parsley, or almonds. Chill several hours. Yield: 3 dozen.

Cooked Salad Dressing

2 egg yolks, lightly beaten
2 tablespoons vinegar
1 tablespoon butter or margarine
1 tablespoon sugar
⅛ teaspoon salt
⅛ teaspoon pepper
⅛ teaspoon red pepper
⅛ teaspoon celery seeds
⅛ teaspoon dry mustard

Combine all ingredients in a small saucepan; cook over medium heat, stirring constantly, until thickened. Cool. Yield: ¼ cup.

CHILDREN'S PARTY SANDWICHES

1 (3-ounce) package cream cheese,
    softened
¼ cup raisins
¼ cup dry-roasted unsalted peanuts
1 tablespoon milk
    Dash of ground cinnamon
24 slices thin sliced wheat bread
1 cherry-flavored chewy rolled fruit
    snack

Position knife blade in food processor bowl; add first 5 ingredients. Top with cover and process until smooth, scraping sides of processor bowl occasionally.

Cut bread into 24 desired Christmas shapes, making a matching pair of each shape to be put together as a sandwich. Spread about 1 tablespoon filling on 1 side of each of 12 pieces of bread; top with matching shaped bread. Unroll fruit snack; slice into 12 thin strips and tie a bow on each sandwich. Yield: 1 dozen.

BUTTER COOKIES

½ cup butter or margarine, softened
1 cup sugar
1 egg
1 teaspoon vanilla extract
3 cups all-purpose flour
¼ teaspoon baking soda
¼ cup commercial sour cream
⅔ cup green candy coating pieces,
    melted
⅔ cup pink candy coating pieces,
    melted

Cream butter; gradually add sugar, beating at medium speed of an electric mixer. Add egg and vanilla; beat well.

Combine flour and soda; add to creamed mixture alternately with sour cream, beating just until blended. Shape dough into two 12-inch rolls; wrap in wax paper and chill at least 2 hours.

Unwrap rolls and cut into ¼-inch slices; place on lightly greased cookie sheets. Bake at 350° for 8 to 10 minutes. Cool slightly on cookie sheets; remove to wire racks to cool completely.

Dip one end of half the cookies in green candy coating, and place on wax paper-lined cookie sheet; refrigerate 5 minutes or until coating is hardened. Repeat procedure with remaining cookies and pink candy coating. Yield: 7½ dozen.

CHOCOLATE MADELEINES

2 eggs
⅛ teaspoon salt
½ cup sugar
½ teaspoon vanilla extract
½ cup all-purpose flour
2 tablespoons cocoa
½ cup butter or margarine, melted
2 ounces chocolate-flavored candy coating, melted
2 ounces vanilla-flavored candy coating, melted

Beat eggs and salt in a medium mixing bowl at high speed of an electric mixer until foamy. Gradually add sugar and vanilla; beat at high speed 15 minutes. Combine flour and cocoa; fold into egg mixture 2 tablespoons at a time. Fold butter into egg mixture, 1 tablespoon at a time.

Spoon 1 tablespoon batter into greased and floured madeleine molds; bake at 400° for 8 to 10 minutes. Cool in molds 3 minutes. Remove from molds and cool on a wire rack, flat side down. Drizzle ridged side with chocolate- and vanilla-flavored candy coating; let coating harden before serving or storing. Yield: about 2 dozen.

PECAN CUPS

8 sheets commercial frozen phyllo pastry, thawed
  Butter-flavored vegetable cooking spray
3 tablespoons butter
¼ cup plus 2 tablespoons sugar
¼ cup plus 2 tablespoons light corn syrup
2 eggs, beaten
½ teaspoon vanilla extract
1 cup chopped pecans

Place 1 sheet of phyllo on a towel or wax paper (keep remaining phyllo covered).

Spray phyllo with cooking spray. Layer 3 more sheets of phyllo on first sheet, spraying each with cooking spray. Repeat to make another stack of 4 sheets of phyllo. Cut each stack of phyllo into 3-inch squares, using kitchen shears.

Spray miniature muffin pans with cooking spray. Place one square of layered phyllo into each muffin cup, pressing gently in center to form a pastry shell.

Combine butter, sugar, and corn syrup; cook over low heat, stirring constantly, until sugar dissolves. Let cool 10 minutes. Add eggs, vanilla, and chopped pecans to mixture; mix well.

Pour filling evenly into prepared phyllo cups. Bake at 325° for 20 minutes or until golden brown. Yield: 40 pastries.

SPICE COOKIES

1½ cups butter or margarine, softened
1 cup firmly packed brown sugar
1 egg, lightly beaten
1½ teaspoons vanilla extract
3½ cups all-purpose flour
1 teaspoon baking powder
1 teaspoon ground cinnamon
1 teaspoon ground cloves
1 teaspoon ground ginger
  Candied cherry halves

Cream butter; gradually add sugar, beating at medium speed of an electric mixer until light and fluffy. Add egg and vanilla; beat well.

Combine flour and next 4 ingredients; gradually add to creamed mixture, mixing until blended. Place dough in a large decorator bag fitted with tip No. 6B. Pipe dough into stars onto ungreased cookie sheets. Place a candied cherry half on top of each cookie. Bake at 375° for 8 to 10 minutes. Yield: 8 dozen.

Entertain with Ease and Style

Cement your reputation as a hostess who makes stylish entertaining look effortless. This menu for a Christmas buffet is filled with unusual and festive dishes that you either prepare ahead or pull together quickly with your microwave.

At a time when heavy foods are the rule, a Seafood Casserole entrée is a delightful switch. Lemony Broccoli and Company Salad with Raspberry Vinaigrette complement the seasonings in the casserole wonderfully. Then the delectable finale comes in a beautiful Holiday Sorbet.

Currant-Jalapeño Pepper Jelly
with Cream Cheese and Crackers
Seafood Casserole
Lemony Broccoli
Company Salad with
Raspberry Vinaigrette
Holiday Sorbet

101

CURRANT-JALAPEÑO PEPPER JELLY

4 (12-ounce) jars red currant jelly
¼ cup seeded, diced jalapeño pepper
¼ cup vinegar

Spoon jelly into a large saucepan; cook over low heat, stirring until jelly melts. Add pepper and vinegar. Bring to a boil; reduce heat to low and simmer 5 minutes. Skim off foam with a metal spoon. Pour mixture into hot sterilized jars; wipe jar rims. Cover with metal lids and screw on bands; refrigerate up to 3 months. Serve with turkey, ham, lamb, pork, or with cream cheese and crackers. Yield: 8 half pints.

SEAFOOD CASSEROLE

1 cup dry white wine
1 tablespoon butter or margarine
1 tablespoon chopped fresh parsley
1 teaspoon salt
1 medium onion, thinly sliced
1 pound fresh bay scallops
1 pound fresh medium shrimp,
  peeled and deveined
3 tablespoons butter or margarine
3 tablespoons all-purpose flour
1 cup half-and-half
½ cup (2 ounces) shredded Swiss
  cheese
2 teaspoons lemon juice
⅛ teaspoon pepper
½ pound seafood mix
1 (4-ounce) can sliced mushrooms,
  drained
1 cup soft breadcrumbs
¼ cup freshly grated Parmesan
  cheese
  Chopped fresh parsley
  Paprika
3 whole cooked shrimp, peeled and
  deveined (optional)

Above: Currant-Jalapeño Pepper Jelly is a versatile condiment you'll enjoy throughout the holidays. Served with cream cheese and crackers, it is a make-ahead appetizer that eases last-minute preparations. Going one step further, put out jars of the jelly, topped with tiny brightly decorated grapevine wreaths, for party favors.

Combine first 5 ingredients in a Dutch oven; bring to a boil. Add scallops and shrimp and cook 3 to 5 minutes; drain, reserving ⅔ cup liquid.

Melt 3 tablespoons butter in a Dutch oven over low heat; add flour, stirring until smooth. Cook 1 minute, stirring constantly. Gradually add half-and-half; cook over medium heat, stirring constantly, until mixture is thickened and bubbly. Add Swiss cheese, stirring until cheese melts. Gradually stir in reserved liquid, lemon juice, and pepper; add scallop mixture, seafood mix, and mushrooms. Spoon mixture into a lightly greased 12- x 8- x 2-inch baking dish. Cover and refrigerate 8 hours.

Remove baking dish from refrigerator and let stand 30 minutes at room temperature. Bake, covered, at 350° for 40 minutes. Combine breadcrumbs and Parmesan cheese; sprinkle evenly over seafood mixture and bake an additional 5 minutes. Sprinkle with parsley and paprika; let stand 10 minutes before serving. Garnish with whole shrimp, if desired. Yield: 8 servings.

Microwave Directions: Combine first 7 ingredients in a 12- x 8- x 2-inch baking dish. Cover tightly with plastic wrap; fold back a small edge of wrap to allow steam to escape. Microwave at HIGH 4 to 6 minutes or until shrimp are done, stirring at 2 minute intervals. Let stand 3 minutes; drain, reserving ⅔ cup liquid.

Place 3 tablespoons butter in a 1-quart glass measure. Microwave at HIGH 45 seconds or until melted. Add flour, stirring until smooth. Gradually add half-and-half, stirring well. Microwave at HIGH 3 to 4 minutes or until thickened and bubbly, stirring after 2 minutes, then at 1-minute intervals. Add Swiss cheese, stirring until cheese melts. Stir in reserved liquid, lemon juice, and pepper; add scallop mixture, seafood mix, and mushrooms. Spoon mixture back into the 12- x 8- x 2-inch baking dish. Cover with plastic wrap and refrigerate 8 hours.

Remove baking dish from refrigerator and let stand 30 minutes at room temperature.

Fold back a small edge of wrap to allow steam to escape and microwave at HIGH 10 minutes or until thoroughly heated, stirring once. Combine breadcrumbs and Parmesan cheese; sprinkle evenly over seafood mixture. Let stand 10 minutes. Sprinkle with parsley and paprika. Garnish with whole shrimp, if desired.

LEMONY BROCCOLI

  2 pounds fresh broccoli
¼ cup water
¼ cup butter or margarine, cut into small pieces
  3 tablespoons lemon juice
  1 teaspoon dried whole basil
½ teaspoon salt
¼ teaspoon pepper
  8 lemon rind rings

Trim off large leaves of broccoli and remove tough ends of lower stalks. Wash broccoli thoroughly and cut into spears. Arrange broccoli in a 12- x 8- x 2-inch baking dish, stem ends out; add water. Cover tightly with plastic wrap; fold back a small edge of wrap to allow steam to escape. Microwave at HIGH 7 to 8 minutes or just until tender; drain. Add butter and next 4 ingredients; toss gently. Arrange broccoli spears in lemon rind rings. Yield: 8 servings.

Tip: Use finely chopped fresh herbs whenever possible. Dried whole herbs are usually the next best choice since they maintain their strength longer than the commercially ground form. Remember to use 3 times more fresh herbs in a recipe if it calls for the more potent dried form.

COMPANY SALAD
WITH RASPBERRY VINAIGRETTE

1 head Bibb lettuce, torn into
   bite-size pieces
½ pound fresh spinach, torn into
   bite-size pieces
2 oranges, peeled and sectioned
2 red apples, unpeeled and thinly
   sliced
1 kiwifruit, thinly sliced
½ cup coarsely chopped walnuts,
   toasted
   Raspberry Vinaigrette

Combine first 6 ingredients in a large
bowl. Toss with Raspberry Vinaigrette. Yield:
8 servings.

Raspberry Vinaigrette

½ cup walnut or vegetable oil
¼ cup raspberry vinegar
1 tablespoon honey
½ teaspoon grated orange rind
¼ teaspoon salt
⅛ teaspoon pepper

Combine all ingredients in a jar; cover
tightly and shake vigorously. Chill thoroughly. Yield: ¾ cup.

HOLIDAY SORBET

1 (12-ounce) package fresh or frozen
   cranberries
1½ cups orange juice
1 cup water
⅔ cup sugar
2 tablespoons Grand Marnier or
   other orange-flavored liqueur
   (optional)
1¾ cups water
¼ cup plus 2 tablespoons sugar
1½ teaspoons lemon juice
1 (6-ounce) can frozen limeade
   concentrate, undiluted

Combine first 4 ingredients in a large
saucepan; bring to a boil. Cover, reduce
heat, and simmer 6 to 8 minutes or until
cranberry skins pop; cool 10 minutes. Position knife blade in food processor bowl. Add
half of cranberry mixture; process until
smooth. Repeat procedure with remaining
mixture. Strain mixture, discarding pulp;
stir in Grand Marnier, if desired. Pour into a
13- x 9- x 2-inch pan; freeze until firm, stirring several times during freezing process.

Combine 1¾ cups water and ¼ cup plus 2
tablespoons sugar in a saucepan; cook over
medium heat until sugar dissolves, stirring
constantly. Remove from heat and add
lemon juice and limeade concentrate; stir
until limeade melts. Pour mixture into an
8-inch square pan; freeze until firm, stirring
several times during freezing process.

Position knife blade in processor bowl.
Add half of frozen cranberry mixture; process until smooth. Repeat procedure with
remaining mixture. Spoon one batch of the
mixture into a 9- x 5- x 3-inch loafpan,
spreading evenly. Set remaining batch aside.

Position knife blade in processor bowl.
Add lime mixture; process until smooth.
Spoon over cranberry mixture in pan,
spreading evenly. Spoon remaining cranberry mixture on top; spread evenly. Cover
and freeze until firm. Remove from pan; cut
into slices. Garnish as desired and serve
with commercial cookies. Yield: 8 servings.

This page: Holiday Sorbet is a sweet ending to a satisfying meal, but its lightness leaves the palate refreshed. Sandwiching a lime sorbet between cranberry layers repeats the colors of the season, and garnishes of fresh mint leaves and cranberries complete the effect.

A Bountiful Christmas Brunch

The excitement of giving and receiving burns calories! Renew your loved ones' energy Christmas morning with a bountiful brunch of ham, grits, fruit, and breads. A few changes give these familiar dishes a surprising freshness.

Orange-Baked Ham
Gruyère Grits
Fruit in Grapefruit Cups
Whole Wheat Biscuits
Raisin Bread
Breakfast Tea
Christmas Coffee

ORANGE-BAKED HAM

1 (1-inch-thick) smoked fully cooked
   ham steak (about 2 pounds)
1 cup orange juice
1 teaspoon whole cloves
1 cup ginger ale
3 tablespoons brown sugar
2 tablespoons orange marmalade
1 tablespoon cornstarch
½ teaspoon dry mustard
½ teaspoon grated orange rind
⅛ teaspoon ground ginger

Place ham in a shallow baking dish. Set aside.

Combine orange juice and cloves in a small saucepan; bring to a boil. Remove from heat and cool. Remove and discard cloves; stir in ginger ale. Pour 1 cup juice mixture over ham; refrigerate remaining 1 cup mixture to make sauce. Cover and chill 8 hours, turning ham occasionally.

Remove ham from marinade, reserving marinade. Place ham on rack of a shallow roasting pan; bake at 325° for 25 minutes or until meat thermometer registers 140°, basting twice with marinade. Discard remaining marinade.

Combine reserved 1 cup juice mixture, brown sugar, and remaining ingredients in a small saucepan. Bring to a boil, stirring constantly; reduce heat, and simmer 1 minute.

Brush ham with 2 tablespoons sauce and broil 4 inches from heat 4 to 5 minutes. Slice ham into ¼-inch slices and serve with remaining sauce. Yield: 6 servings.

GRUYÈRE GRITS

4 cups water
1 teaspoon salt
1 cup uncooked regular grits
1½ cups (6 ounces) shredded Gruyère
    or Swiss cheese
3 tablespoons grated Parmesan
    cheese
½ teaspoon salt
½ teaspoon pepper
¼ teaspoon garlic powder
¼ teaspoon dry mustard
3 egg yolks, lightly beaten
⅓ cup half-and-half
½ cup (2 ounces) shredded Gruyère
    or Swiss cheese
¼ cup grated Parmesan cheese
    Paprika (optional)

Combine water and 1 teaspoon salt in a large saucepan; bring to a boil. Stir in grits; cook until done, following package directions. Remove from heat; add 1½ cups Gruyère cheese and next 5 ingredients, stirring until cheese melts.

Combine egg yolks and half-and-half; stir into grits mixture. Pour mixture into a lightly greased 10- x 6- x 2-inch baking dish; cover and refrigerate 8 hours.

Remove baking dish from refrigerator, and let stand at room temperature 30 minutes. Bake, uncovered, at 350° for 30 minutes. Sprinkle with ½ cup Gruyère cheese and ¼ cup Parmesan cheese; bake an additional 5 minutes. Sprinkle with paprika, if desired. Yield: 6 servings.

Microwave Directions: Combine water, salt, and grits in a 3-quart glass bowl. Microwave at HIGH 14 to 16 minutes, stirring after 7 minutes. Add 1½ cups Gruyère cheese and next 5 ingredients, stirring until cheese melts.

Combine egg yolks and half-and-half; stir into grits mixture. Pour mixture into a lightly greased 10- x 6- x 2-inch baking dish; cover and refrigerate 8 hours.

Remove baking dish from refrigerator, and let stand at room temperature 30 minutes. Microwave, uncovered, at HIGH 15 to 17 minutes. Sprinkle with ½ cup Gruyère and ¼ cup Parmesan cheese and let stand 10 minutes. Sprinkle with paprika, if desired.

FRUIT IN GRAPEFRUIT CUPS

3 grapefruits
6 (12-inch) orange rind strips
1 (8-ounce) can pineapple chunks
3 oranges, peeled and sectioned
1 cup sliced strawberries
½ pound seedless green grapes
¼ cup lime juice
3 tablespoons honey

Cut each grapefruit in half horizontally. To make handle, mark ½-inch-wide segments at two opposite sides of the cut surface. Starting halfway between marked segments, slice around fruit, parallel to surface and ¼-inch below it, stopping at ½-inch segments. Carefully remove and section pulp; set aside. Repeat procedure with remaining grapefruit halves. Gently lift the opposite sides of the ¼-inch rind to form handles; tie together with orange rind strips. Place in an airtight container; chill 8 hours.

Drain pineapple, reserving 2 tablespoons juice. Combine pineapple, reserved grapefruit pulp, and remaining fruit. Combine 2 tablespoons pineapple juice, lime juice, and honey; pour over fruit, tossing to coat. Cover and chill 8 hours. Using a slotted spoon, place fruit mixture in grapefruit cups. Yield: 6 servings.

WHOLE WHEAT BISCUITS

    1 cup whole wheat flour
    1 cup all-purpose flour
    2 teaspoons baking powder
    ¼ teaspoon baking soda
    ½ teaspoon salt
    ⅓ cup butter-flavored shortening
    1 egg, beaten
    1 tablespoon honey
    ¾ cup buttermilk

Combine wheat flour, all-purpose flour, baking powder, baking soda, and salt; cut in shortening with a pastry blender until mixture resembles coarse meal.

Combine egg, honey, and buttermilk. Add buttermilk mixture to flour mixture, stirring until dry ingredients are moistened. Turn dough out onto a lightly floured surface and knead 4 or 5 times.

Roll dough to ½-inch thickness; cut with a 2-inch biscuit cutter. Place on a lightly greased baking sheet. Bake at 450° for 8 to 10 minutes. Yield: 16 biscuits.

RAISIN BREAD

    1 package dry yeast
    ½ cup warm water (105° to 115°)
    ¼ cup sugar
    1 teaspoon salt
    1 teaspoon grated orange rind
    1 cup butter, softened
    6 eggs
    4½ cups all-purpose flour, divided
    1 cup golden raisins
    1½ cups sifted powdered sugar
    ½ teaspoon rum flavoring
    1 to 2 tablespoons water

Dissolve yeast in warm water; let stand 5 minutes. Combine yeast mixture, sugar, salt, orange rind, butter, eggs, and 2 cups flour in a large mixing bowl. Beat at low speed of an electric mixer until well blended; continue beating 4 minutes at medium speed. Stir in remaining 2½ cups flour until well blended. Stir in raisins.

Cover and let rise in a warm place (85°), free from drafts, 1½ to 2 hours or until doubled in bulk. Punch dough down; cover and refrigerate at least 8 hours.

Turn dough out onto a lightly floured surface. Shape dough into an 18-inch rope; pinch ends together, forming a ring. Place ring in a well-greased and floured 10-inch Bundt pan. Cover and let rise in a warm place (85°), free from drafts, 1 hour or until dough has doubled in bulk. Bake at 350° for 45 minutes or until loaf sounds hollow when tapped. Remove loaf from pan, and let cool on a wire rack.

Combine powdered sugar, rum flavoring, and 1 tablespoon water, stirring well. Add enough of the remaining tablespoon water for desired consistency. Drizzle over loaf. Yield: one 10-inch loaf.

CHRISTMAS COFFEE

    1 (3-inch) stick cinnamon
    7 whole cloves
    7 cups water
    ¼ cup sugar
    ¼ cup plus 2 tablespoons instant
        coffee granules
        Whipped cream
        Chocolate sprinkles

Tie cinnamon stick and cloves in a cheesecloth bag. Combine water, sugar, and spice bag in a Dutch oven; bring to a boil. Remove from heat.

Remove spice bag from liquid, and stir in coffee granules. Pour into cups; top with whipped cream and chocolate sprinkles. Serve immediately. Yield: 7 cups.

108

This page: Pamper your clan on Christmas morning with savory and nourishing Raisin Bread. It's especially good served with Breakfast Tea, which is flavored with citrus and spices.

BREAKFAST TEA

½ teaspoon whole cloves
½ teaspoon whole allspice
2 (3-inch) sticks cinnamon
2 cups water
3 regular-size tea bags
½ cup sugar
3 cups white grape juice
2 cups orange juice
¼ cup lemon juice
   Orange slices (optional)

Combine cloves, allspice and cinnamon sticks in a cheesecloth bag; set spice mixture aside.

Bring water to a boil in a large saucepan; add tea bags. Remove from heat; cover and steep 5 minutes. Remove tea bags, squeezing gently. Add spice mixture, sugar, and white grape, orange, and lemon juices. Bring to a boil; cover, reduce heat, and simmer 5 minutes. Remove spices, and serve hot. Garnish with orange slices, if desired. Yield: 7½ cups.

Beverages

COFFEE GROG

2 tablespoons butter or margarine, softened
1 cup firmly packed brown sugar
¼ teaspoon ground cinnamon
¼ teaspoon ground nutmeg
⅛ teaspoon ground allspice
⅛ teaspoon ground cloves
  Light rum (optional)
  Hot coffee
  Sweetened whipped cream
  Ground cinnamon

Cream butter; gradually stir in sugar and spices. Spoon mixture into an airtight container; refrigerate.

To serve, place 1 tablespoon spice mixture and, if desired, 1 tablespoon rum in a large mug; add 1 cup coffee and stir well. Top with whipped cream and sprinkle with cinnamon. Yield: 16 servings.

AFTER-DINNER CREAM

1 teaspoon instant coffee granules
2 tablespoons hot water
2 cups half-and-half
1 (14-ounce) can sweetened condensed milk
¾ cup bourbon
1 teaspoon vanilla extract

Dissolve coffee granules in hot water. Combine coffee and remaining ingredients in container of an electric blender; blend until smooth. Chill. Yield: 5 cups.

COFFEE EGGNOG

2 cups milk
¾ cup water
2 eggs, separated
⅓ cup sugar
3 tablespoons instant coffee granules
  Dash of salt
1 tablespoon vanilla extract
2 tablespoons sugar
1 cup whipping cream, whipped
  Grated unsweetened chocolate

Place milk and water in top of a double boiler; bring water to a boil. Cook until milk is thoroughly heated.

Beat egg yolks at medium speed of an electric mixer until frothy. Add ⅓ cup sugar, coffee granules, and salt, beating until thick. Gradually stir about one-fourth of hot mixture into yolk mixture; add to remaining hot mixture, stirring constantly. Cook in double boiler over low heat 30 minutes, stirring occasionally. Stir in vanilla; cover and chill.

Beat egg whites (at room temperature) until soft peaks form; gradually add 2 tablespoons sugar, beating until stiff peaks form. Fold egg whites and whipped cream into chilled mixture. Sprinkle each serving with grated chocolate. Yield: 5½ cups.

COFFEE ICE-CREAM SMOOTHIE

3 cups coffee ice cream
¼ cup Frangelica or hazelnut-flavored liqueur
¼ cup Cognac
  Ice cubes

Combine all ingredients, except ice, in container of an electric blender. Add enough ice cubes to make mixture measure 4 cups in blender. Blend until smooth. Serve immediately. Yield: 1 quart.

BRANDY SLUSH

  2 cups boiling water
  1 family-size tea bag
  1 (12-ounce) can frozen lemonade
      concentrate, thawed and
      undiluted
  1 (12-ounce) can frozen orange juice
      concentrate, thawed and
      undiluted
  7 cups water
  1 cup sugar
  1 cup brandy

Pour 2 cups boiling water over tea bag; cover and steep 5 minutes. Remove tea bag, squeezing gently. Stir in remaining ingredients and freeze until firm. To serve, partially thaw mixture. Yield: 3½ quarts.

HOT FRUITED TEA PUNCH

  2 or 3 (3-inch) sticks cinnamon
  1 tablespoon whole cloves
  1 quart water
  2 family-size tea bags
1½ to 2 cups sugar
  4 quarts water
  1 quart orange juice
  1 quart apple juice
  1 (48-ounce) jar cranapple juice
  1 (46-ounce) can pineapple juice
1¼ cups lemon juice

Combine cinnamon sticks and cloves in a cheesecloth bag; set aside.
Bring 1 quart water to a boil in a large kettle; add spice mixture and tea bags. Remove from heat; cover and steep 30 minutes. Remove tea bags and spices. Add sugar and remaining ingredients. Cook over low heat, stirring occasionally, until sugar dissolves and mixture is thoroughly heated. Yield: 2½ gallons.

CRANBERRY PUNCH

  1 quart cranberry juice cocktail
  1 quart pineapple juice
  ¼ cup sugar
  2 teaspoons almond extract
  2 (33.8-ounce) bottles ginger ale,
      chilled

Combine first 4 ingredients; stir until sugar dissolves. Chill. To serve, pour juice mixture into punch bowl; gently stir in ginger ale. Yield: 1 gallon.

Above: When friends drop by for a yuletide visit, serve them something tasty to drink, like the Brandy Slush, Cranberry Punch, and Coffee Grog shown here.

111

This page: Christmas brings out the best in cooks, especially those who are bakers. Shown here are Chunky Chocolate Bread, Lemon Bowknots, and Raisin-Filled Pastries.

Breads

CHUNKY CHOCOLATE BREAD

½ cup water
¼ cup butter or margarine
¼ cup sugar
1 package dry yeast
¼ cup warm water (105° to 115°)
3 to 3½ cups all-purpose flour, divided
3 tablespoons cocoa
¾ teaspoon salt
⅛ teaspoon ground cinnamon
2 eggs
1 teaspoon vanilla extract
½ cup semisweet chocolate chunks
Glaze (recipe follows)

Combine ½ cup water, butter, and sugar in a saucepan; heat until butter melts. Cool to 105° to 115°.

Dissolve yeast in ¼ cup warm water in a large mixing bowl; let stand 5 minutes. Add butter mixture, 2 cups flour, cocoa, salt, cinnamon, eggs, and vanilla; beat at low speed of an electric mixer 30 seconds. Beat an additional 3 minutes at medium speed. Gradually stir in enough remaining flour to make a soft dough.

Turn dough out onto a floured surface and knead until smooth and elastic (about 8 to 10 minutes). Place in a well-greased bowl, turning to grease top. Cover and let rise in a warm place (85°), free from drafts, 1 hour or until doubled in bulk.

Punch dough down and turn out onto a floured surface; roll into an 18- x 10-inch rectangle; sprinkle with chocolate chunks, pressing chunks gently into dough. Roll up dough, jellyroll fashion, starting at one short end. Fold ends under and place seam side down in a greased 9- x 5- x 3-inch loafpan. Cover and let dough rise in a warm place, free from drafts, for 45 minutes or until loaf has doubled in bulk.

Bake at 350° for 30 minutes or until loaf sounds hollow when tapped. Remove bread from pan immediately; cool on a wire rack. Drizzle glaze over loaf. Yield: 1 loaf.

Glaze

1 cup sifted powdered sugar
1½ tablespoons milk
½ teaspoon vanilla extract

Combine all ingredients, stirring well. Yield: about ⅓ cup.

HONEY-BRAN MUFFINS

2 cups whole bran cereal
1 cup shreds of wheat bran cereal
½ cup boiling water
2½ cups all-purpose flour
1½ teaspoons baking soda
½ cup shortening
1 cup honey
2 eggs, beaten
2 cups buttermilk
Honey Butter

Combine cereals; add water, stirring well. Set aside.

Combine flour and soda in a large bowl; make a well in center of mixture.

Combine shortening and honey; add eggs and buttermilk, stirring until blended. Stir in cereal mixture; add to dry ingredients, stirring just until moistened.

Spoon into paper-lined muffin pans, filling three-fourths full. Bake at 350° for 25 minutes or until done. Remove from pans immediately. Serve with Honey Butter. Yield: 2½ dozen.

Honey Butter

1 (8-ounce) jar honey
½ cup butter or margarine, softened

Combine honey and butter, stirring until blended. Yield: 1 cup.

RAISIN-FILLED PASTRIES

2 (8-ounce) packages cream cheese, softened
1 cup butter, softened
1 cup margarine, softened
6 cups all-purpose flour
Powdered sugar
Filling (recipe follows)

Combine first 3 ingredients in a large mixing bowl; beat at medium speed of an electric mixer until mixture is smooth. Add flour and mix well.

Divide dough into fourths. Roll out one portion into a 12- x 9-inch rectangle on a surface sprinkled lightly with powdered sugar; cut into 12 (3-inch) squares. Spoon about 2 teaspoons filling onto each square, leaving a ½-inch margin. Roll squares jellyroll fashion, and place seam side down on ungreased baking sheets; bake at 375° for 20 to 22 minutes or until lightly browned. Cool on wire racks. Repeat procedure with remaining dough and filling. Yield: 4 dozen.

Filling

¾ cup raisins
1¼ cups hot water
1½ cups ground pecans
¾ cup sugar
1½ teaspoons ground cinnamon

Combine raisins and water; let stand 15 minutes. Drain.

Combine raisins and remaining ingredients. Yield: 2⅔ cups.

Note: Pastries may be sealed in an airtight container and frozen before baking. Thaw at room temperature; bake as directed above.

LEMON BOWKNOTS

1 cup milk
⅓ cup sugar
½ cup shortening
1 teaspoon salt
1 package dry yeast
¼ cup warm water (105° to 115°)
2 eggs, beaten
¼ cup milk
1 tablespoon grated lemon rind
5 to 5½ cups all-purpose flour, divided
1 cup sifted powdered sugar
1 to 2 tablespoons milk
1 teaspoon grated lemon rind

Combine first 4 ingredients in a saucepan; heat until shortening melts. Cool to 105° to 115°.

Dissolve yeast in warm water in a large bowl; let stand 5 minutes. Add milk mixture, eggs, ¼ cup milk, 1 tablespoon lemon rind, and 3 cups flour to yeast; beat at medium speed of an electric mixer until smooth. Gradually stir in enough remaining flour to make a soft dough. Cover and let stand 10 minutes.

Turn dough out onto a lightly floured surface, and knead until smooth and elastic (about 5 minutes). Place in a well-greased bowl, turning to grease top. Cover and let rise in a warm place (85°), free from drafts, 1 to 1½ hours or until doubled in bulk.

Punch dough down; cover and let stand 15 minutes. Roll dough into an 18- x 10-inch rectangle. Cut dough into twenty-four 10- x ¾-inch strips. Roll each strip back and forth lightly in hands to make a rope; tie loosely into a knot. Place on greased baking sheets. Cover and let rise in a warm place, free from drafts, 35 minutes or until doubled in bulk. Bake at 400° for 10 to 12 minutes or until golden brown.

Combine powdered sugar, 1 tablespoon milk, and 1 teaspoon lemon rind, stirring well. Add more milk, if needed, to make glaze desired consistency. Brush glaze on bowknots. Yield: 2 dozen.

CRANBERRY COFFEE CAKE

- 1 cup milk
- ½ cup commercial sour cream
- ½ cup butter or margarine
- ½ cup sugar
- 2 packages dry yeast
- ½ cup warm water (105° to 115°)
- 2 eggs, beaten
- 2 teaspoons salt
- 2 teaspoons grated orange rind
- 5½ to 6 cups all-purpose flour, divided
- 1 (14-ounce) jar cranberry-orange relish
- 2 tablespoons chopped pecans
- 1 cup sifted powdered sugar
- 1 tablespoon orange juice

Combine first 4 ingredients in a saucepan; heat until butter melts. Cool to 105° to 115°.

Dissolve yeast in warm water in a large bowl; let stand 5 minutes. Add milk mixture, eggs, salt, orange rind, and 2 cups flour to yeast; beat at medium speed of an electric mixer 2 minutes. Gradually stir in enough remaining flour to make a stiff dough. Place dough in a well-greased bowl, turning to grease top; cover and refrigerate for at least 8 hours.

Turn dough out onto a lightly floured surface and knead until smooth and elastic (about 1 minute). Roll dough into a 15- x 10-inch rectangle on a lightly floured surface. Spread relish evenly over dough, leaving a 1-inch margin; sprinkle with pecans.

Roll up dough, jellyroll fashion, starting at one long side; pinch seam to seal. Place roll on a large greased baking sheet, seam side down; shape into a ring and pinch ends together to seal.

Using kitchen shears, make cuts in dough at 1-inch intervals around ring, cutting two-thirds of the way through roll with each cut. Gently turn each piece of dough on its side, slightly overlapping slices.

Cover dough and let rise in a warm place (85°), free from drafts, 45 minutes or until doubled in bulk. Bake at 375° for 20 minutes or until golden brown. Transfer to a wire rack. Combine powdered sugar and orange juice; drizzle over coffee cake while warm. Yield: 1 coffee cake.

Above: A Cranberry Coffee Cake adds seasonal flavor to the coffee klatch. For fresh, hot bread in the morning, prepare the dough ahead and store it overnight in the refrigerator.

115

WHOLE WHEAT BUTTERHORNS

2½ cups whole wheat flour, divided
2 packages dry yeast
2 teaspoons salt
1¾ cups water
3 tablespoons butter or margarine
⅓ cup honey
2 to 2½ cups all-purpose flour
¼ cup plus 2 tablespoons butter, softened and divided
¼ cup plus 2 tablespoons chopped pecans, divided (optional)
Butter or margarine, melted

Combine 1½ cups whole wheat flour, yeast, and salt in a large mixing bowl. Combine water, 3 tablespoons butter, and honey in a saucepan; heat until butter melts, stirring occasionally. Cool to 120° to 130°.

Gradually add liquid mixture to flour mixture, beating at high speed of an electric mixer 3 minutes. Gradually stir in remaining 1 cup wheat flour and enough all-purpose flour to make a stiff dough.

Turn dough out onto a lightly floured surface and knead until smooth and elastic (about 5 to 7 minutes). Place in a well-greased bowl, turning to grease top. Cover and let rise in a warm place (85°), free from drafts, 1 hour or until doubled in bulk.

Punch dough down and divide into thirds. Roll each into a 12-inch circle on a floured surface; spread each with 2 tablespoons butter and sprinkle each with 2 tablespoons chopped pecans, if desired. Cut each circle into 12 wedges; roll up each wedge, beginning at wide end. Place on greased baking sheets, point side down.

Cover and let rise in a warm place, free from drafts, 30 minutes or until doubled in bulk. Bake at 400° for 10 minutes or until golden brown. Brush with melted butter. Yield: 3 dozen.

ORANGE BISCUITS

2 cups self-rising flour
3 tablespoons sugar
1 teaspoon grated orange rind
1 cup whipping cream
Orange Filling
Butter or margarine, melted

Combine first 4 ingredients, stirring with a fork until blended. Turn dough out onto a lightly floured surface and knead 10 to 12 times.

Roll dough into a 12- x 8-inch rectangle; spread with Orange Filling. Roll up jellyroll fashion, starting at long side. Pinch seam and ends together. Slice roll into 1-inch pieces and place in greased and floured muffin pans. Bake at 425° for 15 to 20 minutes. Remove from pans immediately and brush with melted butter. Yield: 1 dozen.

Orange Filling

¼ cup butter or margarine
1 tablespoon plus ¾ teaspoon all-purpose flour
¼ cup orange juice
1½ teaspoons grated orange rind
¼ cup sugar

Melt butter in a heavy saucepan; add flour and cook 1 minute, stirring constantly. Gradually add orange juice; cook over medium heat until thickened. Stir in grated orange rind and sugar. Chill mixture thoroughly. Yield: ⅔ cup.

Cakes and Pies

ANGEL FOOD COCONUT CAKE

12 egg whites
1 teaspoon cream of tartar
½ teaspoon salt
1 cup sugar
1 cup all-purpose flour
1 teaspoon vanilla extract
   Fluffy White Frosting
2 cups grated fresh or frozen
   coconut

Beat egg whites (at room temperature) at medium speed of an electric mixer until foamy. Add cream of tartar and salt; beat until soft peaks form. Add sugar, 2 tablespoons at a time, beating until stiff peaks form. Sprinkle flour over mixture, ¼ cup at a time; fold in carefully. Fold in vanilla.

Pour batter into an ungreased 10-inch tube pan, spreading evenly. Bake at 375° for 30 to 35 minutes or until cake springs back when lightly touched. Invert pan; cool 40 minutes. Loosen cake from sides of pan using a narrow metal spatula; remove from pan. Spread top and sides with Fluffy White Frosting; sprinkle with coconut. Yield: one 10-inch cake.

Fluffy White Frosting

1⅓ cups sugar
⅔ cup water
2 egg whites
½ teaspoon coconut extract

Combine sugar and water in a heavy saucepan. Cook over medium heat, stirring constantly, until clear. Cook, without stirring, to soft ball stage (240°).

Beat egg whites (at room temperature) until soft peaks form; continue to beat, slowly adding syrup mixture. Add coconut extract; continue beating until stiff peaks form and frosting is thick enough to spread. Yield: 4 cups.

BOURBON CAKE

1½ cups butter or margarine, softened
2 cups sugar
1 cup firmly packed brown sugar
6 eggs
5 cups all-purpose flour, divided
1 teaspoon baking powder
2 teaspoons ground nutmeg
1 cup bourbon
1 cup milk
1 pound (about 2 cups) red and
   green candied cherries
1 (8-ounce) package whole pitted
   dates, chopped
4 cups chopped pecans

Make a liner for a 10-inch tube pan by drawing a circle with an 18-inch diameter on a piece of brown paper. (Do not use recycled paper.) Cut out circle; set pan in center, and draw around base of pan and inside tube. Fold circle into eighths, having the drawn lines on the outside.

Cut off tip end of circle along inside drawn line. Unfold paper; cut along folds from outside edge to lines drawn around base of pan. Cut another circle with a 10-inch diameter; grease and set aside. Place the 18-inch liner in pan; grease and flour. Set aside.

Cream butter and sugars at medium speed of an electric mixer until light and fluffy. Add eggs, one at a time, beating after each addition. Combine 4 cups flour, baking powder, and nutmeg; add to creamed mixture, alternately with bourbon and milk, beginning and ending with flour mixture. Mix after each addition.

Combine candied cherries, dates, and pecans. Dredge in remaining 1 cup flour. Fold mixture into batter.

Spoon batter into prepared pan. Cover pan with greased 10-inch brown paper circle, placing greased side down. Bake at 275° for 4 hours. Take off paper, and bake an additional 30 minutes. Cool completely on a wire rack. Remove cake from pan; peel away paper liner. Yield: one 10-inch cake.

WHITE CHOCOLATE ROULAGE

4 eggs, separated
¾ cup sugar, divided
1 tablespoon vegetable oil
1 teaspoon vanilla extract
⅔ cup sifted cake flour
1 teaspoon baking powder
¼ teaspoon salt
1 to 2 tablespoons powdered sugar
  White Chocolate Cream Filling
  White chocolate curls

Lightly oil bottom and sides of a 15- x 10- x 1-inch jellyroll pan with vegetable oil; line with wax paper and lightly oil and flour wax paper. Set aside.

Beat egg yolks at high speed of an electric mixer until foamy. Gradually add ¼ cup sugar, beating until mixture is thick and lemon colored (about 5 minutes). Stir in vegetable oil and vanilla; set aside.

Beat egg whites (at room temperature) until foamy; gradually add remaining ½ cup sugar, beating until whites are stiff but not dry. Fold whites into yolks. Combine flour, baking powder, and salt; gradually fold into egg mixture. Spread batter evenly into prepared pan. Bake at 350° for 8 to 10 minutes.

Sift powdered sugar in a 15- x 10-inch rectangle on a cloth towel. When cake is done, immediately loosen from sides of pan, and turn out onto sugared towel. Carefully peel off wax paper. Starting at narrow end, roll up cake and towel together; let cake cool completely on a wire rack, seam side down.

Unroll cake. Spread cake with half of White Chocolate Cream Filling and carefully reroll cake, without towel. Place cake on a serving plate, seam side down; spread remaining filling on all sides. Garnish with white chocolate curls. Yield: 8 to 10 servings.

Preceding pages: White Chocolate Roulage . . . just the idea of it stops conversation. But when it is revealed in all its glory, expect to hear cries of delight.

White Chocolate Cream Filling

1½ teaspoons unflavored gelatin
3 tablespoons cold water
1 (6-ounce) white chocolate-flavored baking bar, grated
1¼ cups whipping cream
1 teaspoon vanilla extract

Sprinkle gelatin over water in a small saucepan; let stand 1 minute. Cook over low heat, stirring until gelatin dissolves. Add grated baking bar and stir constantly until chocolate melts; cool slightly.

Combine whipping cream and gelatin mixture in a mixing bowl; beat at medium speed of an electric mixer until thickened. Stir in vanilla. Chill. Yield: 3 cups.

GINGERBREAD POUND CAKE

1 cup butter or margarine, softened
1 cup sugar
5 eggs
2 cups all-purpose flour
½ teaspoon baking soda
1 teaspoon ground ginger
1 teaspoon ground cinnamon
1 teaspoon ground cloves
1 cup molasses
½ cup commercial sour cream
  Sifted powdered sugar
  Lemon Sauce (optional)

Cream butter; gradually add sugar, beating well at medium speed of an electric mixer. Add eggs, one at a time, beating after each addition.

Combine flour, soda, and spices; set aside. Combine molasses and sour cream. Add flour mixture to creamed mixture alternately with molasses mixture, beginning and ending with flour mixture. Mix just until blended after each addition.

Pour batter into a greased and floured 10-inch Bundt pan. Bake at 325° for 1 hour or until a wooden pick inserted in center comes out clean. Cool in pan 15 minutes; remove from pan and let cool completely on a wire rack. Sprinkle with powdered sugar. Serve with Lemon Sauce, if desired. Yield: one 10-inch cake.

Lemon Sauce

- ½ cup sugar
- 2 tablespoons cornstarch
- 1 cup water
- 1 tablespoon butter or margarine
- 2 teaspoons grated lemon rind
- ⅓ cup lemon juice

Combine first 3 ingredients in a saucepan, stirring until smooth. Cook over medium heat, stirring until smooth and thickened. Add remaining ingredients; cook until heated. Yield: 1⅔ cups.

CREAM CHEESE BROWNIE CAKE

- ⅓ cup shortening
- ¾ cup sugar
- 1 egg
- 1 cup all-purpose flour
- ½ teaspoon baking powder
- ½ teaspoon salt
- ⅓ cup cocoa
- ½ cup water
- 1 envelope unflavored gelatin
- ¼ cup water
- 2 (8-ounce) packages cream cheese, softened
- ½ cup sugar
- 1½ teaspoons lemon juice
- ½ teaspoon vanilla extract
- 2 egg whites
- 3 (1-ounce) squares semisweet chocolate
- 1 teaspoon shortening
- 1 cup whipping cream
- 2 tablespoons powdered sugar
- 1 teaspoon vanilla extract
- 13 large maraschino cherries

Cream ⅓ cup shortening; gradually add ¾ cup sugar, beating well at medium speed of an electric mixer. Add egg, beating well.

Combine next 4 ingredients; add to creamed mixture alternately with ½ cup water, beginning and ending with flour mixture. Pour batter into a greased 9-inch springform pan. Bake at 350° for 25 minutes or until a wooden pick inserted in center comes out clean. Cool on a wire rack.

Sprinkle gelatin over ¼ cup water in a small saucepan; let stand 1 minute. Cook over low heat, stirring until gelatin dissolves. Remove from heat.

Beat cream cheese at medium speed of an electric mixer until fluffy. Add ½ cup sugar, lemon juice, ½ teaspoon vanilla, and gelatin, mixing well.

Beat egg whites (at room temperature) at high speed of an electric mixer until stiff peaks form. Fold into cheese mixture. Spoon mixture on top of chocolate layer. Cover and chill until set.

Melt chocolate and 1 teaspoon shortening in a small saucepan over low heat, stirring constantly. Draw a 9-inch circle on a piece of wax paper. Place wax paper on a baking sheet. Spread chocolate evenly on circle. Chill until partially set (about 7 minutes). Using a pizza wheel or sharp knife, cut chocolate into 12 wedges. Chill until firm.

Beat whipping cream until foamy; gradually add powdered sugar and 1 teaspoon vanilla, beating until soft peaks form.

Run a spatula around sides of springform pan, release clasp, and remove sides of pan. Carefully transfer cake to a serving plate; remove bottom of pan. Frost top and sides of cake with whipped cream, reserving about 1 tablespoon for garnish. Place 12 cherries evenly around outer edges of cake about ½-inch from edge. Peel a chocolate wedge carefully from wax paper and prop against cherry with point of wedge in center of cake, anchoring the outer edge in whipped cream. Continue process with remaining chocolate wedges. Dollop reserved whipped cream in center and place remaining cherry on top. Yield: 12 servings.

Above: After a special dinner, serve your guests Cranberry-Orange Cream Tarts and Bourbon Cake, with piping hot coffee. That way you'll be covered, whether they prefer a fruity and light dessert, a sweet and rich one, or both!

CRANBERRY-ORANGE CREAM TARTS

Pastry for three 9-inch piecrusts
1 **cup sugar, divided**
1 **envelope unflavored gelatin**
¼ **cup water**
1 **teaspoon grated orange rind**
1 **tablespoon orange juice**
1 **cup finely chopped fresh**
   cranberries
3 **egg whites**
¼ **teaspoon cream of tartar**
1 **cup whipping cream, whipped**
   Orange rind strips (optional)
   Whole fresh cranberries (optional)

Divide pastry into thirds; roll out each portion on a lightly floured surface to ⅛-inch thickness; cut each portion into five 4½-inch circles. Fit circles into 4-inch fluted tart pans. Prick bottoms and sides of tart shells with a fork; bake at 450° for 9 to 11 minutes or until lightly browned. Cool.

Combine ⅔ cup sugar and gelatin in a small saucepan; stir in water, orange rind, orange juice, and cranberries. Cook over medium heat until mixture boils, stirring constantly. Remove from heat. Chill until consistency of unbeaten egg whites.

Beat egg whites (at room temperature) and cream of tartar at high speed of an electric mixer 1 minute. Gradually add remaining ⅓ cup sugar, 1 tablespoon at a time, beating until stiff peaks form and sugar dissolves (2 to 4 minutes). Fold beaten egg whites and whipped cream into cranberry mixture. Spoon mixture evenly into tart shells. Cover and chill at least 1 hour. If desired, garnish with orange rind strips and whole fresh cranberries. Yield: 15 tarts.

PUMPKIN-RAISIN-RUM PIE

½ cup raisins
¼ cup rum
¼ cup water
¾ cup firmly packed brown sugar
1 tablespoon all-purpose flour
½ teaspoon salt
½ teaspoon ground cinnamon
½ teaspoon ground ginger
¼ teaspoon ground nutmeg
¼ teaspoon ground cloves
1 (16-ounce) can pumpkin
2 eggs, beaten
1 cup evaporated milk
1 unbaked 9-inch pastry shell
   Sweetened whipped cream
      (optional)

Combine raisins, rum, and water in a small bowl; let stand 20 minutes.

Combine brown sugar, flour, salt, and spices in a large bowl, stirring well. Add raisin mixture, pumpkin, eggs, and milk, stirring well. Pour filling into pastry shell. Bake at 450° for 20 minutes; reduce heat to 350°, and bake an additional 30 minutes or until set. Cool. Top with dollops of whipped cream, if desired. Yield: one 9-inch pie.

CRUSTY MERINGUE-PECAN PIE

3 egg whites
1 cup sugar
1 cup chopped pecans
1 cup round buttery cracker crumbs
1 teaspoon vanilla extract
¾ cup whipping cream
2 tablespoons powdered sugar
¼ cup chopped pecans, toasted

Beat egg whites (at room temperature) at high speed of an electric mixer 1 minute. Gradually add sugar, 1 tablespoon at a time, beating well. Fold in 1 cup pecans, cracker crumbs, and vanilla. Spoon into a lightly greased 9-inch pieplate; bake at 325° for 25 to 30 minutes or until pie is set. Cool on a wire rack.

Beat whipping cream and powdered sugar until soft peaks form. Dollop around edge of pie and sprinkle with toasted pecans. Yield: one 9-inch pie.

Note: After baking, pie will have a crusty, meringue-like top.

MACADAMIA CHRISTMAS PIE

2 (3½-ounce) jars macadamia nuts
⅓ cup flaked coconut
1 unbaked 9-inch pastry shell
4 eggs, lightly beaten
1 cup light corn syrup
½ cup sugar
¼ teaspoon salt
1½ teaspoons vanilla extract
½ cup whipping cream
1½ tablespoons cream of coconut

Rinse macadamia nuts with hot water; drain well and pat dry with paper towels. Coarsely chop nuts.

Press coconut onto bottom and sides of unbaked pastry shell; set aside.

Combine eggs and next 4 ingredients; stir in macadamia nuts. Pour filling into prepared pastry shell. Bake at 350° for 15 minutes. Reduce temperature to 325° and bake an additional 35 minutes or until filling is set. Cool.

Beat whipping cream until soft peaks form; stir in cream of coconut. Dollop mixture on top of each serving of pie. Yield: one 9-inch pie.

Cookies and Candies

DATE-FILLED COOKIES

- 1 cup shortening
- ½ cup sugar
- ½ cup firmly packed brown sugar
- 1 egg
- 3 tablespoons milk
- 1 teaspoon vanilla extract
- 3 cups all-purpose flour
- ½ teaspoon baking soda
- ½ teaspoon salt
- 1 cup chopped dates
- ¼ cup sugar
  Pinch of salt
- ¼ cup water
- 1 tablespoon lemon juice

Cream shortening; gradually add sugars, beating well at medium speed of an electric mixer. Add egg, milk, and vanilla, mixing well. Combine flour, soda, and salt; gradually add dry ingredients to creamed mixture, mixing well.

Use a cookie press to shape dough into 2-inch flowers. (Using a small paring knife, lift center circle from half the flowers.) Bake at 375° for 10 to 12 minutes. Remove to wire racks and cool completely.

Combine dates and next 3 ingredients; bring to a boil. Cover, reduce heat, and simmer 5 minutes, stirring occasionally. Add lemon juice. Cool.

Just before serving, turn half the cookies bottom up and spread each with 1 teaspoon filling. Place a second cookie, with center part removed, on top of filling (top side up). Yield: 3 dozen.

GINGERBREAD COOKIES

- ½ cup shortening
- ½ cup sugar
- ½ cup molasses
- ¼ cup water
- 2½ cups all-purpose flour
- ½ teaspoon salt
- ½ teaspoon baking soda
- ¾ teaspoon ground ginger
- ½ teaspoon ground cinnamon
- ¼ teaspoon ground cloves
  Glaze (recipe follows)
  Assorted candies

Cream shortening; gradually add sugar, beating at medium speed of an electric mixer until light and fluffy. Add molasses and water and beat well. Combine flour, salt, soda, and spices; add to creamed mixture, beating well. Cover and chill 8 hours.

Divide dough in half; store 1 portion in refrigerator. Roll other portion to ¼-inch thickness on a lightly floured surface. Cut with a 3-inch cookie cutter and place on ungreased cookie sheets. Bake at 375° for 8 minutes. Cool 2 minutes. Remove to wire racks and cool completely. Repeat procedure with remaining dough.

Using a small paintbrush, paint assorted designs with glaze on cookies. Decorate with assorted candies. Yield: about 4 dozen.

Glaze

- 2 cups sifted powdered sugar
- 2 tablespoons lemon juice
- 2 tablespoons water
  Paste food coloring

Combine sugar, juice, and water. Tint as desired with paste food coloring. Yield: about ⅔ cup.

Opposite: Make your little ones proud this year by serving their friends Gingerbread Cookies in playful shapes and colors.

QUICK CRISPY COOKIES

    1   cup butter or margarine, softened
    ½   cup firmly packed brown sugar
    1¾ cups all-purpose flour
    ½   teaspoon ground cinnamon
    ¼   teaspoon ground nutmeg
    ¼   teaspoon ground allspice
    ⅛   teaspoon ground cloves
    1½ cups crushed corn flake cereal
    1   cup finely chopped pecans
    1½ teaspoons vanilla extract
        Powdered sugar

Cream butter at medium speed of an electric mixer; gradually add sugar, beating until light and fluffy.

Combine flour and spices; add to creamed mixture, mixing well. Stir in corn flakes, pecans, and vanilla. Shape mixture into 1-inch balls and place 1-inch apart on greased cookie sheets. Bake at 350° for 15 to 20 minutes or until lightly browned.

Remove to wire racks and cool completely. Sprinkle with powdered sugar. Yield: about 4½ dozen.

VIENNESE COOKIES

    1½ cups all-purpose flour
    ¼   cup sugar
    ¾   cup butter, well chilled and cut
        into 1-inch pieces
    1   tablespoon commercial sour
        cream
    1   teaspoon vanilla extract
    24 pecan halves, candied cherry
        halves, or milk chocolate kisses

Position knife blade in food processor bowl; add flour and sugar. Top with cover and pulse 3 or 4 times or until combined. Add butter to flour mixture. Pulse 5 or 6 times or until mixture resembles coarse meal. With processor running, add sour cream and vanilla; process only until dough begins to form a ball and leaves the sides of the bowl. Cover and chill 30 minutes.

Shape dough into 24 balls; place each in a greased 1¾-inch muffin pan and gently press a pecan half into center of each. Bake at 350° for 22 to 25 minutes. Remove from pans and cool on wire racks. Yield: 2 dozen.

ORANGE SHORTBREAD

    1   cup butter, softened
    ¾   cup sifted powdered sugar
    1   teaspoon grated orange rind
    2   teaspoons orange juice
        concentrate, thawed and
        undiluted
    1¾ cups all-purpose flour
        Pecan halves or sliced almonds

Cream butter; gradually add powdered sugar, beating at medium speed of an electric mixer until light and fluffy. Add orange rind and concentrate. Stir in flour.

Press dough into a lightly greased 15- x 10- x 1-inch jellyroll pan; prick all over with a fork. Cut into 1½-inch diamonds. Place a pecan half in center of each diamond. Bake at 300° for 30 minutes or until done. Re-cut diamonds while warm. Let cool in pan. Yield: about 4 dozen.

CAPPUCCINO CANDY

1 tablespoon instant coffee granules
1 tablespoon hot water
2 cups sugar
1 cup evaporated milk
½ cup butter or margarine
1 (12-ounce) package semisweet
    chocolate morsels
1 (7-ounce) jar marshmallow cream
1 cup chopped pecans
1 tablespoon grated orange rind
2 teaspoons orange juice or orange
    extract
2 teaspoons brandy extract

Combine coffee granules and water, stirring until granules dissolve. Set aside.

Combine sugar, milk, and butter in a large saucepan. Cook over medium heat until mixture comes to a boil, stirring constantly; boil 10 minutes, stirring constantly. Remove from heat.

Add chocolate morsels and marshmallow cream, stirring until melted. Stir in coffee mixture, pecans, and remaining ingredients. Spread mixture evenly in a greased 13- x 9- x 2-inch pan. Cover and chill; cut into squares. Store in refrigerator. Yield: 2¾ pounds.

COFFEE DIVINITY

½ cup boiling water
1 tablespoon instant coffee granules
2½ cups sugar
½ cup light corn syrup
2 egg whites
1 teaspoon vanilla extract

Combine water and coffee granules in a 3-quart saucepan, stirring until coffee dissolves. Add sugar and corn syrup; cook over low heat, stirring gently, until sugar dissolves. Cover and cook over medium heat 2 to 3 minutes to wash down sugar crystals from sides of pan. Uncover and cook over medium heat, without stirring, to hard ball stage (260°). Remove from heat.

Beat egg whites (at room temperature) until stiff peaks form. Pour hot mixture in a very thin stream over egg whites while beating constantly at high speed of an electric mixer. Add vanilla and continue beating just until mixture holds its shape (3 to 4 minutes). Drop by rounded teaspoonfuls onto wax paper. Let cool. Yield: 3 dozen.

CHOCOLATE-DIPPED COCONUT CREAMS

1 (14-ounce) can sweetened
    condensed milk
¼ cup butter or margarine, melted
1 tablespoon lemon juice
8 cups sifted powdered sugar
1 (7-ounce) can flaked coconut
½ cup chopped almonds, toasted
16 ounces chocolate-flavored candy
    coating

Combine first 3 ingredients; stir well. Gradually stir in powdered sugar. Add coconut and almonds, mixing well; shape into ¾-inch balls. Cover and freeze 4 hours or until firm.

Place candy coating in top of a double boiler; bring water to a boil. Reduce heat to low; cook until coating melts. Remove from heat, leaving coating over hot water. Using two forks, dip frozen candy pieces in melted coating, allowing excess to drip off; cool on wax paper. Store in refrigerator. Yield: 8 dozen.

This page: If you set out holiday treats, you want them to be as pretty as they are tasty. Take a look at these confections. From front, Meringue Trees with Chocolate Buttercream, Christmas Mints, and Date-Filled Cookies.

MERINGUE TREES
WITH CHOCOLATE BUTTERCREAM

2¼ cups sifted powdered sugar
3 egg whites
   Green paste food coloring
   Chocolate Buttercream

Line two large baking sheets with un-glazed brown paper. Sketch 24 (3½-inch-long) Christmas trees onto paper. Set aside.

Combine powdered sugar and egg whites in top of a double boiler. Beat at low speed of an electric mixer 30 seconds or just until blended.

Place over boiling water; beat constantly on high speed 5 to 7 minutes or until stiff peaks form. Remove from heat.

Fit tip No. 22 (or another medium-size fluted tip) into decorating bag. Using a small art brush, paint about a ¼-inch-wide stripe of food coloring inside bag from tip end to outer edge. Carefully spoon meringue mixture into bag; close bag securely. Starting at top of tree and using a zigzag motion, pipe trees. Bake at 300° for 25 minutes. Remove from oven; cool on baking sheets. Carefully peel away paper. Store in an airtight container at room temperature up to 2 days.

Before serving, pipe or spread Chocolate Buttercream on flat sides of half the meringue trees; top with remaining meringue trees. Yield: 1 dozen.

Chocolate Buttercream

⅓ cup butter or margarine, softened
¾ cup plus 2 tablespoons sifted powdered sugar
1½ tablespoons cocoa
½ teaspoon vanilla extract
1 to 2 teaspoons milk

Cream butter at medium speed of an electric mixer; gradually add sugar, beating until light and fluffy. Add cocoa, vanilla, and enough milk to make mixture a good spreading consistency; beat well. Yield: about ⅔ cup.

CHRISTMAS MINTS

½ cup butter or margarine, softened
1 (16-ounce) package powdered sugar, sifted
2 tablespoons milk
2 tablespoons finely crushed hard peppermint candy
⅛ teaspoon oil of peppermint
   About 20 (2-ounce) squares chocolate-flavored candy coating
   Decorator Frosting (recipe follows)

Cream butter; gradually add sugar, beating well. Stir in next 3 ingredients, mixing well. Divide into 4 portions; shape each into a ball. Roll out each portion to ¼-inch thickness; cut with a 1-inch round cutter. Place on cookie sheets; cover and chill.

Place candy coating in top of a double boiler; bring water to a boil. Reduce heat to low; cook until coating melts, stirring often. Remove from heat, leaving coating over hot water. Dip chilled mints in coating to cover all sides, allowing excess to drip. Place on wax paper-lined cookie sheets. Chill until coating hardens.

Pipe green decorator frosting on mints, using tip No. 65, to make holly leaves, and pipe red frosting, using tip No. 2, to make holly berries. (No. 2 tip can also be used to make trees, stockings, wreaths, and candles.) Yield: 8 dozen.

Decorator Frosting

3 tablespoons butter or margarine, softened
2 cups sifted powdered sugar
2 tablespoons milk
½ teaspoon vanilla extract
   Red and green paste food coloring

Cream butter and sugar until light and fluffy. Add milk and vanilla, beating to spreading consistency. Divide in thirds; color one-third of the frosting red and the remaining two-thirds green. Yield: 1¼ cups.

129

CHOCOLATE DESSERT CHEESE

1½ cups raisins
½ cup light or dark rum
3 (8-ounce) packages cream cheese, softened
¾ cup chopped pecans, toasted
1½ cups semisweet chocolate mini-morsels
1 teaspoon ground cinnamon
   Semisweet chocolate shavings or toasted chopped pecans (optional)
   Commercial gingersnap cookies

Soak raisins in rum 3 hours. Drain well, pressing gently between paper towels. Combine cream cheese, ¾ cup pecans, mini-morsels, cinnamon, and raisins in a large bowl, mixing well. (Do not use a mixer.) Cover and chill 1 hour. Shape into a ball and roll in chocolate shavings, if desired. Serve with cookies. Yield: one 6-inch cheese ball.

ORANGE-CRANBERRY LIQUEUR

1 medium-size orange
2 cups fresh cranberries, chopped
2 cups vodka
2 cups sugar

Peel colored rind from orange, leaving inner white portion on fruit. Cut rind into 2- x ¼-inch strips. Squeeze juice from orange.
Combine orange rind, juice, and remaining ingredients in a jar. Cover tightly, and refrigerate 1 month, shaking occasionally.
Strain mixture through 2 layers of cheesecloth. Discard pulp. Store in refrigerator. Yield: 3⅓ cups.

CHOCOLATE MINT TRUFFLES

1 (12-ounce) package semisweet chocolate morsels
4 egg yolks
¼ cup plus 2 tablespoons butter or margarine, cut into cubes
¼ cup plus 2 tablespoons sifted powdered sugar
½ teaspoon mint extract
16 ounces chocolate-flavored candy coating
4 ounces vanilla-flavored candy coating, melted

Place chocolate morsels in top of a double boiler; bring water to a boil. Reduce heat to low; cook until chocolate melts. Remove top of double boiler from hot water.
Beat egg yolks until thick and lemon colored. Gradually stir about one-fourth of hot chocolate into yolks; add to remaining hot mixture, stirring constantly. Add butter, sugar, and mint extract; beat at medium speed of an electric mixer until butter melts and mixture is smooth. Cover with paper towel and let stand in a cool, dry place 1 hour (do not refrigerate).
Shape mixture into ½-inch balls; chill 1 hour or until firm.
Place chocolate candy coating in top of double boiler; bring water to a boil. Reduce heat to low; cook until coating melts. Remove from heat, leaving top of double boiler over hot water. Dip each ball of candy into coating, letting excess coating drip off. Place on wax paper-lined baking sheets and chill until coating hardens. Drizzle truffles with melted vanilla candy coating. Yield: 6 dozen.

Opposite: Make sure you have a witness when you make these Chocolate Mint Truffles for gift-giving. Otherwise no one will believe they aren't from an expensive candy shop. Especially after taking a bite.

HONEY BEAR BREAD

    2 packages dry yeast
    ½ cup warm water (105° to 115°)
    ¼ cup honey
    2 eggs, beaten
    1 tablespoon sugar
    2 teaspoons salt
    ¼ cup vegetable oil
 1½ cups lukewarm water
    2 cups whole wheat flour
    1 cup regular oats, uncooked
 3¼ to 3¾ cups all-purpose flour
    6 raisins
 1½ tablespoons butter or margarine,
        melted

Dissolve yeast in ½ cup warm water in a large mixing bowl; let stand 5 minutes. Stir in honey, eggs, sugar, salt, oil, 1½ cups luke-warm water, and whole wheat flour. Beat at medium speed of an electric mixer until smooth. Stir in oats and enough all-purpose flour to make a soft dough.

Turn dough out onto a floured surface and knead until smooth and elastic (about 8 to 10 minutes). Place in a well-greased bowl, turning to grease top. Cover and let rise in a warm place (85°), free from drafts, 1 hour or until doubled in bulk.

Punch dough down; divide in half. Set one portion aside for second loaf. Divide remaining portion in half. Shape one half into a smooth ball for bear's body and place on a lightly greased baking sheet. Divide remaining half into four equal portions. Shape one of these portions into a round ball and position on baking sheet for bear's head. Shape another portion into two 1-inch balls for ears and attach to head, flattening slightly. Divide and shape remaining two portions into arms and legs and attach to bear's body. Repeat procedure with dough set aside to make second loaf. Position raisins for eyes and noses.

Cover and let rise in a warm place, free from drafts, 20 to 30 minutes or until doubled in bulk. Bake at 350° for 20 to 25 minutes or until loaves sound hollow when tapped. Remove from oven; brush bears with melted butter. Cool on wire racks. Decorate with ribbon, if desired. Yield: 2 loaves.

SOUTHERN PECAN CAKE

    1 cup butter or margarine, softened
    1 cup sugar
    3 eggs
    ¼ cup molasses
    ⅔ cup orange juice
  2¼ cups all-purpose flour
    1 teaspoon baking powder
    1 teaspoon ground nutmeg
    ¾ teaspoon salt
    1 pound (about 3 cups) golden
         raisins
    3 cups chopped pecans
    ¼ pound (about ½ cup) chopped
         candied orange peel
    ½ cup all-purpose flour
         Brandy

Cream butter; gradually add sugar, beating well at medium speed of an electric mixer. Add eggs, one at a time, beating after each addition. Stir in molasses and orange juice.

Combine 2¼ cups flour, baking powder, nutmeg, and salt; add to creamed mixture, beating until blended.

Combine raisins, pecans, and orange peel; dredge in ½ cup flour. Stir into batter.

Spoon batter into a greased and floured 10-inch tube pan. Bake at 275° for 2½ hours or until a wooden pick inserted in center comes out clean. Cool in pan 30 minutes on a wire rack. Remove cake from pan and let cool completely. Wrap cake in brandy-soaked cheesecloth. Store in an airtight container in a cool place. Slice cake with an electric knife. Yield: one 10-inch cake.

ALMOND BISCOTTI

    8 eggs
  1¾ cups sugar
    ¾ cup vegetable oil
    3 cups all-purpose flour
    1 tablespoon baking powder
    ½ teaspoon salt
    1 teaspoon vanilla extract
    ¾ cup whole almonds, coarsely
         ground

Combine eggs, sugar, and oil in a large mixing bowl, beating well at medium speed of an electric mixer. Combine flour, baking powder, and salt; gradually add to egg mixture, beating well. Stir in vanilla. Fold in almonds.

Pour batter into two greased and floured 13- x 9- x 2-inch pans. Bake at 350° for 30 minutes or until a wooden pick inserted in center comes out clean. Cool in pans 10 minutes. Invert cakes onto cooling racks and let cool completely. Cut into 3- x ¾-inch slices. Arrange slices on baking sheets and bake at 350° for 10 to 15 minutes or until crisp and golden brown. Cool completely and store in an airtight container. Yield: 3 dozen.

APPLE-CINNAMON-BRAN MUFFIN MIX

     5 cups all-purpose flour
   2½ cups firmly packed brown sugar
     1 tablespoon plus 2 teaspoons
         baking soda
     1 teaspoon salt
   1½ teaspoons ground cinnamon
     ½ teaspoon ground nutmeg
     1 cup dried cultured buttermilk mix
     1 cup shortening
     1 (15-ounce) package wheat bran
         flakes cereal with raisins
   1½ cups diced dried apples

Combine first 7 ingredients. Cut in shortening with a pastry blender until mixture resembles coarse meal. Stir in cereal and apples. Divide mixture into four equal portions and seal in airtight plastic bags; store in a cool, dry place or in refrigerator up to 6 weeks. Yield: 4 packages mix.

*Gift Card Recipe for
Quick Apple-Cinnamon-Bran Muffins:*

     1 package Apple-Cinnamon-Bran
         Muffin Mix (about 4½ cups)
     1 egg
     1 cup water

Combine 4½ cups muffin mix, 1 egg, and 1 cup water, stirring just until moistened. Spoon evenly into greased muffin pans. Bake at 400° for 15 minutes. Remove from pans immediately. Yield: 1½ dozen.

PARMESAN TOAST STRIPS

     8 slices white bread
     ½ cup crushed corn flakes cereal
     ¼ cup plus 2 tablespoons grated
         Parmesan cheese
     ½ cup butter or margarine, melted
     1 teaspoon onion powder

Remove crust from bread and cut each slice into 5 strips; set aside.

Combine corn flakes and Parmesan cheese. Combine butter and onion powder; brush onto all sides of bread strips. Dredge strips in cereal mixture. Place on ungreased baking sheets; bake at 400° for 9 to 11 minutes or until crisp. Cool on wire racks; store in an airtight container. Yield: 3⅓ dozen.

CHAMPAGNE MUSTARD

     1 cup sugar
     ⅔ cup dry mustard
     3 eggs, beaten
     ⅔ cup white champagne vinegar

Combine sugar and mustard in a heavy saucepan. Add eggs and vinegar; mix well. Cook over low heat, stirring constantly, until thick and smooth. Store in refrigerator. Serve with roast beef or ham. Yield: 1½ cups.

SPICY CURRANT SAUCE

   1¾ cups firmly packed dark brown
         sugar
     3 tablespoons cornstarch
     1 (10-ounce) box currants
     2 cups water
     ⅔ cup red wine vinegar
     ¾ teaspoon ground cinnamon
     ¼ teaspoon ground cloves
     ¼ teaspoon ground allspice
     1 tablespoon grated orange rind

Combine brown sugar and cornstarch in a 2-quart glass bowl; add remaining ingredients, stirring well. Microwave at HIGH 9 to 11 minutes, stirring at 2 minute intervals; let cool. Cover and chill up to 4 weeks. Serve warm with ham or poultry. Yield: 5 cups.

Party Fare

CRANBERRY TURKEY CUPS

- 1 (1-pound) package frozen raw ground turkey, thawed
- ½ cup diced onion
- ¼ cup diced celery
- 1 tablespoon vegetable oil
- ½ cup fine, dry breadcrumbs
- ⅓ cup whole-berry cranberry sauce
- 1 egg, beaten
- 1 teaspoon poultry seasoning
- ½ teaspoon salt
- ½ teaspoon pepper
- 8 sheets commercial frozen phyllo pastry, thawed
  Butter-flavored vegetable cooking spray
- ¼ cup whole-berry cranberry sauce
  Fresh parsley sprigs

Sauté turkey, onion, and celery in hot oil in a large skillet until turkey is browned, stirring to crumble meat. Remove from heat; stir in breadcrumbs, ⅓ cup cranberry sauce, egg, poultry seasoning, salt, and pepper. Set mixture aside.

Place 1 sheet of phyllo pastry on a damp towel (keep remaining phyllo covered). Spray phyllo with cooking spray. Layer 3 more sheets phyllo on first sheet, spraying each with cooking spray. Repeat to make another stack of 4 sheets phyllo. Cut each stack of phyllo into 3-inch squares, using kitchen shears.

Spray miniature muffin pans with cooking spray. Place one square of layered phyllo in each muffin cup, pressing gently in center to form a pastry shell. Fill each shell with one rounded teaspoon turkey mixture. Bake at 350° for 20 to 25 minutes or until golden brown. Top each turkey cup with about ¼ teaspoon cranberry sauce. Garnish with a small sprig of parsley. Serve hot. Yield: about 40 cups.

Above: Most parties end up in the kitchen, but yours will hover near the dishes shown above—Cranberry Turkey Cups, Pesto Dip, and Layered Caviar Spread—until only the parsley remains.

PESTO DIP

- ¾ cup lightly packed fresh basil leaves
- ⅓ cup grated Parmesan cheese
- ¼ cup pine nuts or chopped walnuts, toasted
- 3 tablespoons olive oil
- 1 small clove garlic, minced
- ¼ teaspoon salt
- ¼ teaspoon pepper
- 1 (8-ounce) carton commercial sour cream or sour dressing

Combine first 7 ingredients in container of an electric blender. Process at medium speed until smooth. Stir in sour cream. Serve with fresh vegetables. Yield: 1½ cups.

LAYERED CAVIAR SPREAD

- 1 envelope unflavored gelatin
- ¼ cup cold water
- 8 hard-cooked eggs, peeled and quartered
- ¼ cup mayonnaise
- 2 tablespoons country Dijon mustard
- ¼ cup chopped fresh parsley
- ¼ teaspoon salt
- ¼ teaspoon pepper
- 1 cup green onions, thinly sliced and divided
- 1 (8-ounce) package frozen cooked shrimp, thawed
- 4 (3-ounce) packages cream cheese, softened
- ½ cup cooked, crumbled bacon or bacon bits
- ¼ cup sherry
- ½ cup commercial sour cream
  Chopped fresh parsley
- 1 (2-ounce) jar red caviar, drained
- 1 (2-ounce) jar black caviar, drained
- 1 (2-ounce) jar golden caviar, drained

Sprinkle gelatin over cold water in a small saucepan; let stand 1 minute. Cook over low heat, stirring until gelatin dissolves. Set aside.

Position knife blade in food processor bowl; add hard-cooked eggs. Top with cover and pulse 3 or 4 times. Add 2 tablespoons gelatin mixture, mayonnaise, and next 4 ingredients. Process just until blended. Spoon mixture into a greased 9-inch springform pan; sprinkle with ½ cup green onions. Set aside.

Position knife blade in processor bowl; add shrimp. Top with cover and pulse 3 or 4 times. Add 1 package cream cheese, remaining gelatin mixture, crumbled bacon, and sherry. Process until mixture is smooth; spread over green onions. Sprinkle remaining ½ cup green onions over shrimp mixture. Set aside.

Position knife blade in processor bowl. Add remaining 3 packages cream cheese and sour cream; top with cover and process until mixture is smooth. Spoon over green onions. Cover and chill at least 8 hours.

When ready to serve, remove side of springform pan. Press chopped parsley on top to form a 1-inch border. Arrange caviar on top in 3 equal wedges. Serve with melba toast. Yield: 6 cups.

CRABMEAT FONDUE

- 1 (8-ounce) package cream cheese
- 1 (5-ounce) jar sharp process cheese spread
- 1 (6-ounce) can lump crabmeat, drained and flaked
- ¼ cup half-and-half
- ½ teaspoon Worcestershire sauce
- ¼ teaspoon garlic powder
  Green onion fans
  Paprika
- 1 loaf French bread, cut into 1-inch cubes and toasted
  Boiled shrimp (optional)

Combine cream cheese and cheese spread in a 4-cup glass measure. Microwave at MEDIUM (50% power) 4 minutes, stirring at 2 minute intervals, until cheese melts. Stir in crabmeat, half-and-half, Worcestershire sauce, and garlic powder. Microwave at MEDIUM HIGH (70% power) 2 minutes or until thoroughly heated, stirring at 1 minute intervals. Pour into fondue pot or chafing dish. Garnish with green onion fans and sprinkle with paprika. Serve with French bread cubes and boiled shrimp, if desired. Yield: 2 cups.

CHEESE AND OLIVE APPETIZER

   1 (8-ounce) package Cheddar cheese, cut into ½-inch cubes
   1 (8-ounce) package Monterey Jack cheese, cut into ½-inch cubes
   1 cup pitted ripe olives
   1 (5-ounce) jar pimiento-stuffed olives, drained
   1 (4-ounce) can whole mushrooms, drained
   1 (7¾-ounce) jar golden Greek peppers, drained and cut into ½-inch pieces
   1 (8-ounce) bottle commercial Italian salad dressing
   1 (0.4-ounce) envelope commercial buttermilk salad dressing mix

Combine first 6 ingredients in a large bowl. Combine salad dressing and salad dressing mix in a jar; cover tightly and shake vigorously. Pour dressing mixture over cheese mixture, stirring well. Cover and chill 8 hours. Drain mixture and serve with wooden picks. Yield: 8 cups.

Tip: To keep appetizers appealingly hot—and you out of the kitchen—use your chafing dish and warming trays for serving.

ORANGE DESSERT CHEESE MOLD

   1 (8-ounce) package cream cheese, softened
   ⅓ cup sifted powdered sugar
   1½ tablespoons grated orange rind
   1 tablespoon orange marmalade
   1 tablespoon Grand Marnier (optional)
   ½ cup whipping cream, whipped
   ¼ cup chopped pecans, toasted
       Orange twists (optional)
       Brandysnaps
       Apple wedges

Combine first 5 ingredients, mixing well. Fold whipped cream into cheese mixture. Line a 2-cup mold with several thicknesses of dampened cheesecloth. Spoon cheese mixture into mold, pressing firmly with back of a spoon. Cover and chill at least 8 hours.

Unmold cheese onto a serving plate and remove cheesecloth. Sprinkle cheese with toasted pecans. Garnish with orange twists, if desired. Serve with Brandysnaps and apple wedges. Yield: 2 cups.

Brandysnaps

   ¾ cup shortening
   ¾ cup firmly packed brown sugar
   1 egg
   ¼ cup molasses
   2 tablespoons brandy
   2 cups all-purpose flour
   2 teaspoons baking soda
   ⅛ teaspoon salt
   1 teaspoon ground cinnamon

Cream shortening; gradually add brown sugar, beating at medium speed of an electric mixer until light and fluffy. Add egg, molasses, and brandy; mix well.

Combine last 4 ingredients; stir well. Gradually add flour mixture to creamed mixture, beating until blended. Chill 1 hour. Shape into 1-inch balls; place on ungreased cookie sheets. Bake at 375° for 10 minutes; cool on wire racks. Yield: 4½ dozen.

Yuletide Tips and Traditions

Deck your halls with holly and more! Branch out in new directions and blend some of the South's splendid offerings with traditional favorites. A wide variety of blooming plants, flowers, and bulbs await you, as well as the customary poinsettia, Christmas cactus, and regional varieties of greenery. To help you reap the benefits of an abundant harvest of ornamentals, we've compiled a holiday plant guide, including both the traditional and the more unusual. Here you'll find useful information sprinkled with lore, all guaranteed to add to your appreciation of and skill with the greening of Christmas.

Count on Evergreen For Winning Effects

Evergreen is an ancient symbol of longevity and immortality. The Romans filled their homes with greenery and exchanged holly wreaths as tokens of friendship. Today the ritual is still thriving, with garlands, wreaths, and arrangements galore.

If you properly condition cut greenery, a garland or wreath will stay fresh longer. About 48 hours before you plan to use them, clip notches in the woody ends of branches and place them in a tub of cold water. Then, a few hours before you begin the project, remove the branches from the water and allow to dry.

Poinsettias Have Roots in Mexico

According to legend, a poor Mexican boy sheepishly approached the crèche in his village church on Christmas Eve. It was customary to leave gifts for the Christ Child, but the boy had none to give. As the lad knelt in the snow to pray, a scarlet plant emerged from the frozen ground, and the boy presented it to the babe in the manger. It became known in Mexico as *Flor de la Noche Buena*. In 1928, an American named Joel Roberts Poinsett was visiting Mexico and came across the plant. He brought it back to America where it was renamed for him.

Today, poinsettias are as closely identified with Christmas as holly and mistletoe. For healthy blooms that will endure throughout the holidays, supply poinsettias with bright indirect light and temperatures between 65 and 75 degrees. Feed monthly with water-soluble fertilizer and let the soil go slightly dry between waterings.

To condition for next year's Christmas blooming, first prune off the bracts by early February. Then, plant the poinsettia and its container in a sunny garden after the last spring frost. Cut it back to 18 inches two or three times throughout the summer, making the last cut around September 15. Near the end of October, the plant must receive 14 hours of bright sun during the day and about eight hours of complete darkness at night. After about eight weeks, new bracts should appear; and just in time for the holidays, you can bring the plant back inside to enjoy the color.

Cactus for Christmas

Distinctive with its exotic red, orange, lavender, pink, or white blooms, the Christmas cactus is a boon to plant lovers who claim to be without a "green thumb." The cactus requires a minimum amount of care but yields enchanting results. In fact, the plant is best left alone in bright but indirect sunlight. Feed biweekly with water-soluble 20-20-20 fertilizer and let the soil go slightly dry between waterings.

To ensure a Christmas flowering, set the plant outside in early October when temperatures drop into the upper 40s and 50s. Keep it outdoors for several weeks, until tiny buds form at the tips of the leaves. At that point, take the plant indoors, and it should bloom between Thanksgiving and Christmas. For best results, don't water the plant when it is outside and don't let it freeze. Once you bring the cactus inside, resume the previous watering schedule.

Sneak Preview of Coming Attractions

Colorful blossoms are always a happy surprise in the middle of winter. Whether you force blooms or take advantage of the season's natural offerings, they'll fill your house with scented pleasures. And, a gift that *really* keeps on giving—a flowering plant (given with care and maintenance instructions) will be a reminder of a special friendship throughout the year.

Jerusalem cherry, kalanchoe, and florists' cyclamen bloom in winter, displaying rich green foliage and dramatically contrasting flowers. All of them can be taken outside in the spring and summer and brought indoors the next fall for another blooming.

Many bulbs, such as the amaryllis and paperwhite, can be easily forced to bloom during the holidays, adding an extra splash of color to centerpieces.

To prepare amaryllis bulbs before planting, soak them in lukewarm water for several minutes. In a pot that is slightly larger than the diameter of a bulb, plant the bulb in soil so that about one third of the bulb rises above the soil. Press the soil firmly around the bulb to steady it. For the first few weeks, water sparingly, until the bud and part of the stem have developed. Direct sunlight will help the plant grow properly. When the green sprouts begin to show, more water may be added periodically. The amaryllis takes about six to eight weeks to bloom.

With its slender stems and small flowers, the paperwhite lends itself to forcing in decorative pebbles or in soil. Place in direct sunlight, water regularly, and in four to six weeks, Christmas blooms should appear.

Symbolic Arrangements

Christmas herbs, such as rosemary, thyme, and sage, have long been revered for their flavor and aroma, making them wonderful additions to your wreaths and centerpieces. Rosemary, the symbol of remembrance, once had only white flowers, according to legend. But the Holy Family, during their flight to Egypt, stopped to rest, and Mary washed Baby Jesus' swaddling clothes and her own blue cloak in a running brook. She spread the garments on the branches of a flowering rosemary to dry. When she removed them, they had taken on the fragrance of the herb, and the white flowers had changed to blue.

Firm Foundations

A one-of-a-kind arrangement of fresh flowers and greenery begins with a firm foundation that allows you to keep the materials watered, extending their freshness through the season. Florists' foam is popular because it holds moisture well, but if you insert too many stems, it can crumble. To strengthen it, wrap the block with florists' tape or place it in a wire mesh cage. Woody materials can be anchored with a frog (a metal holder with sharp prongs). Since these materials are often heavy, a slightly off-balance arrangement may fall over. To avoid this, secure the frog to the bottom of the container with florists' clay. All of the above are available from your local variety store or florist's shop.

To keep your cut flowers fresh longer, follow this formula: add 1 can of non-cola soft drink and 1 tablespoon of chlorine bleach to ½ gallon hot water. Cut the stems of the flowers at a diagonal and immediately place them in the water mixture.

Patterns

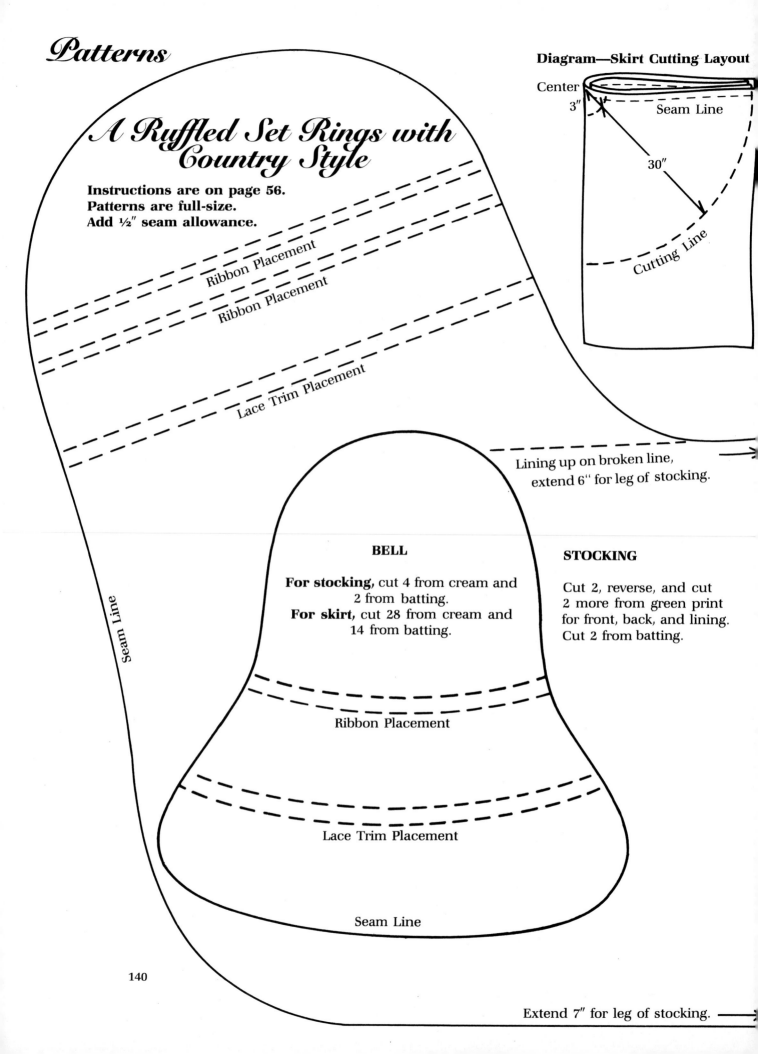

A Ruffled Set Rings with Country Style

Instructions are on page 56.
Patterns are full-size.
Add ½″ seam allowance.

Ribbon Placement

Ribbon Placement

Lace Trim Placement

Center

3″

Seam Line

30″

Cutting Line

Lining up on broken line,
extend 6″ for leg of stocking.

BELL

For stocking, cut 4 from cream and
2 from batting.
For skirt, cut 28 from cream and
14 from batting.

STOCKING

Cut 2, reverse, and cut
2 more from green print
for front, back, and lining.
Cut 2 from batting.

Seam Line

Ribbon Placement

Lace Trim Placement

Seam Line

140

Extend 7″ for leg of stocking.

A Notebook for Christmas Memories

Instructions are on page 64. Cross-Stitch Chart

Fashion Takes a Cue from the Season

CHRISTMAS LIGHTS SWEATSHIRT
Instructions are on page 63.
Patterns are full-size.

PLUG

Cut 1 from gold.

BULB

Cut 5 from red
and 5 from green.

BASE

Cut 10
from gold.

A Glistening Garland Unfolds from Paper

Instructions are on
page 59. Pattern
is full-size.

Place on folds.
Do not cut.

Place on folds.
Do not cut.

Cut circles with
paper punch.

Gingerbread Boys Go Hand in Hand

Instructions are on page 68. Patterns are full-size.
Add ¼″ seam allowance to all pattern pieces. Cross-Stitch Chart

**GINGERBREAD
GARLAND HEART**
Cut 2 from calico.

Half of pattern. Reverse
for other half.

Seam Line

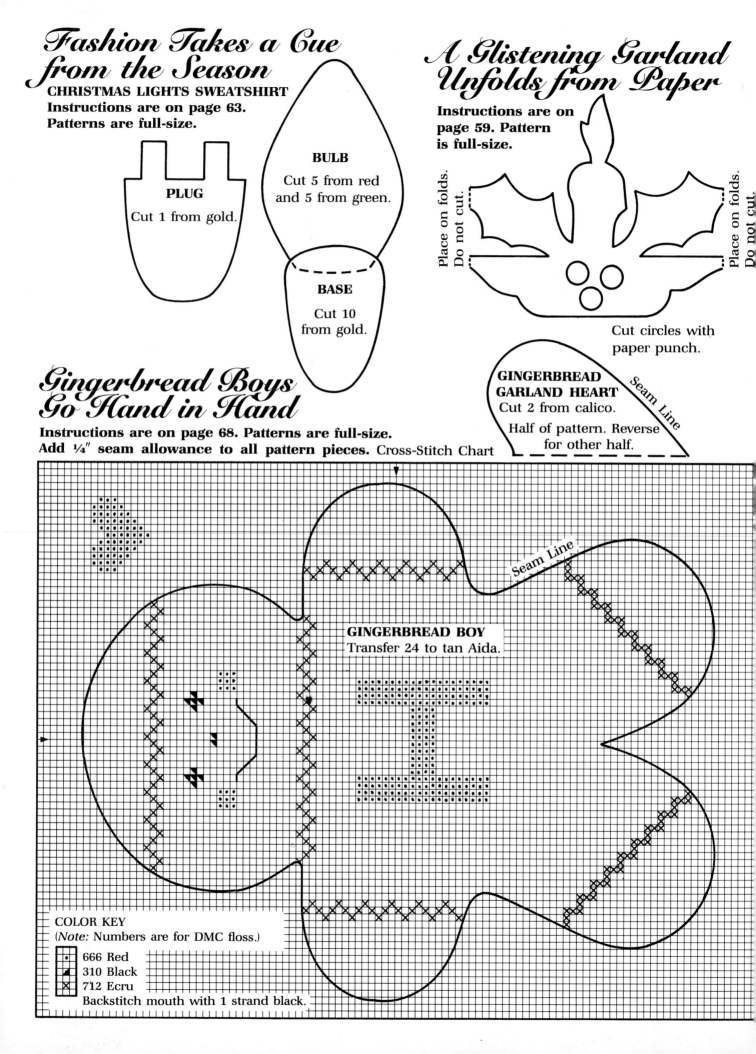

Seam Line

GINGERBREAD BOY
Transfer 24 to tan Aida.

COLOR KEY
(*Note:* Numbers are for DMC floss.)

666 Red
310 Black
712 Ecru
Backstitch mouth with 1 strand black.

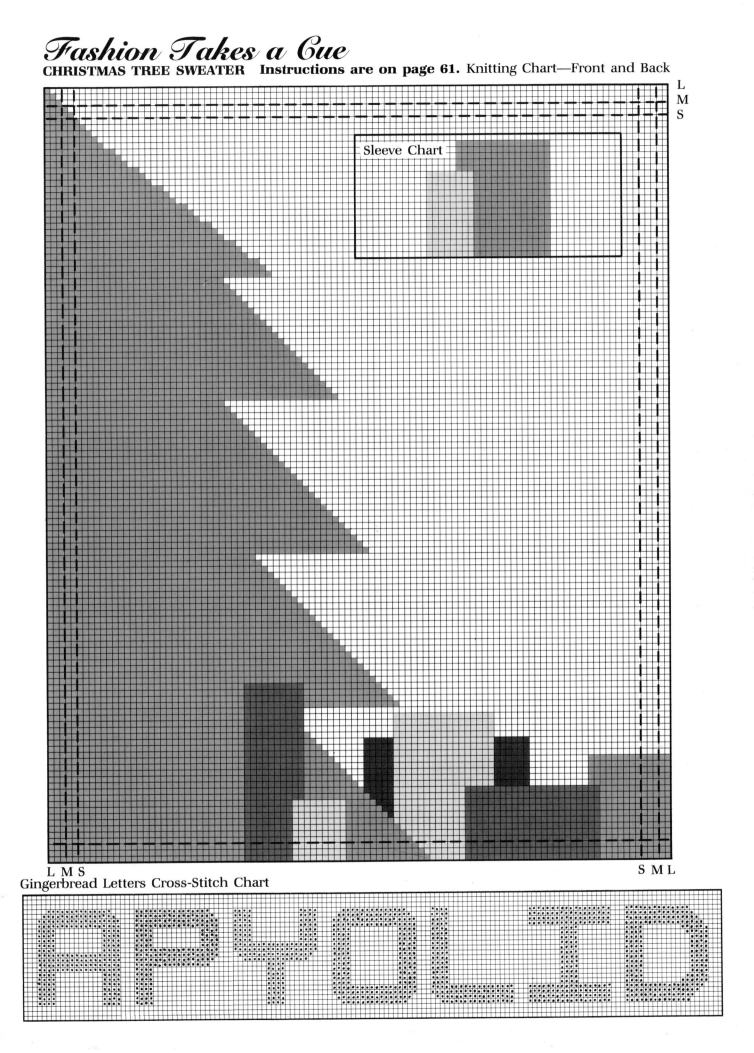

Fashion Takes a Cue

CHRISTMAS TREE SWEATER **Instructions are on page 61.** Knitting Chart—Front and Back

L
M
S

Sleeve Chart

L M S

S M L

Gingerbread Letters Cross-Stitch Chart

The First Christmas in Silhouette

Instructions are on page 67.
Patterns are full-size.

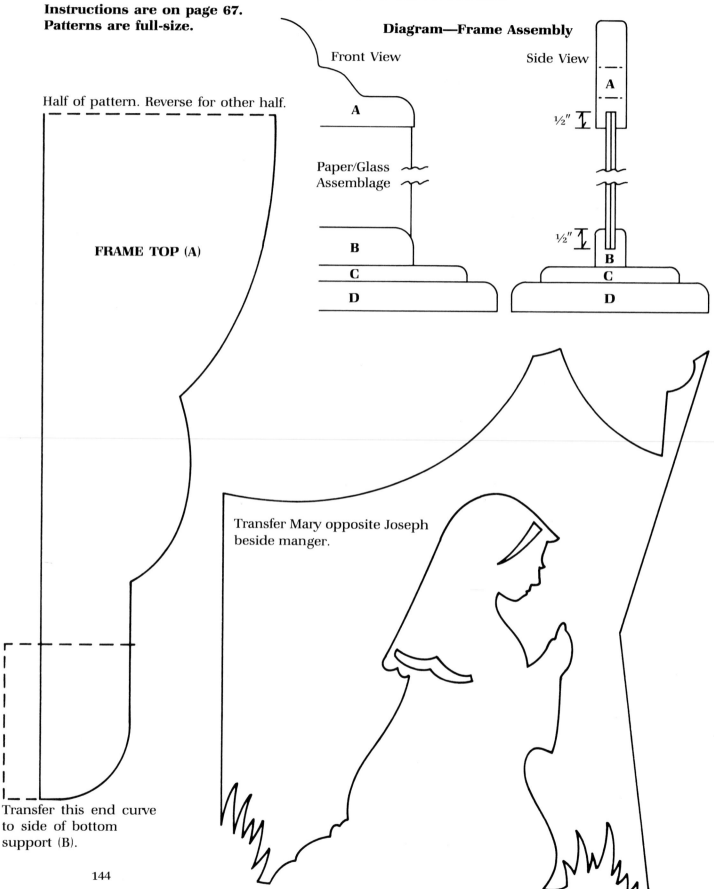

Half of pattern. Reverse for other half.

Diagram—Frame Assembly

Front View

Side View

A

Paper/Glass
Assemblage

FRAME TOP (A)

B

C

D

½"

½"

A

B

C

D

Transfer Mary opposite Joseph
beside manger.

Transfer this end curve
to side of bottom
support (B).

Half of pattern. Reverse and transfer all but Joseph for other half.

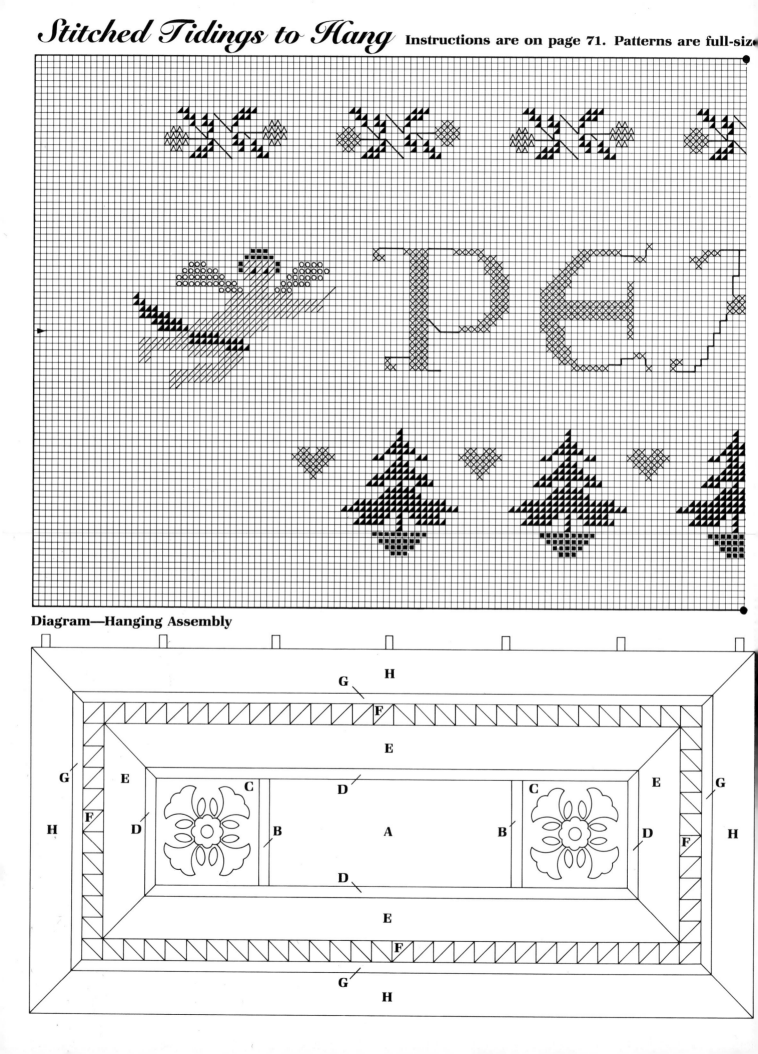

Diagram—Hanging Assembly

and include ¼″ seam allowance. Cross-Stitch Chart

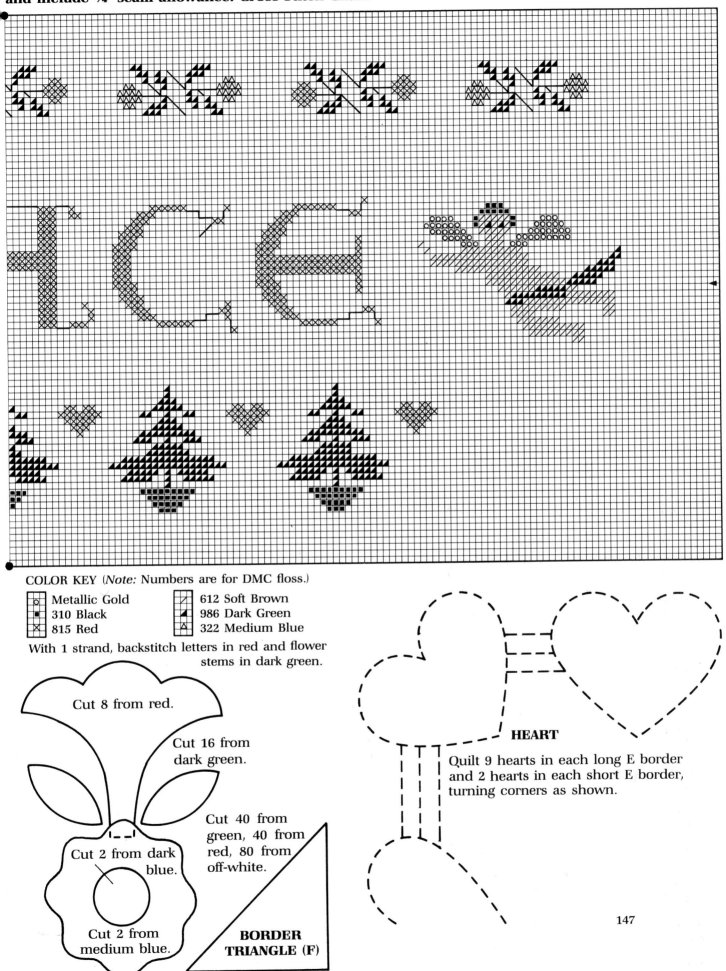

COLOR KEY (*Note:* Numbers are for DMC floss.)

	Metallic Gold		612 Soft Brown
	310 Black		986 Dark Green
	815 Red		322 Medium Blue

With 1 strand, backstitch letters in red and flower stems in dark green.

Cut 8 from red.

Cut 16 from dark green.

Cut 2 from dark blue.

Cut 40 from green, 40 from red, 80 from off-white.

Cut 2 from medium blue.

BORDER TRIANGLE (F)

HEART

Quilt 9 hearts in each long E border and 2 hearts in each short E border, turning corners as shown.

147

Instructions are on page 72.
Patterns are full-size. Add ⅛" seam allowance.

Stitch from
sleeve to here.

DRESS
Cut 2 from red-and-green print.

Seam Line

Place on fold

Ear ✕
Placement

EARS

Cut 1 from
fleece, 1 from
red pindot.

Gather here.

HEAD/BODY
Cut 2 from fleece.

Leave open.

Seam Line

Arm ✕
Placement

Leg Placement ✕
Leave open.

Seam Line

HEART

STOCKING
Cut 2 from
green stripe.

Seam Line

Seam Line

ARM
Cut 4
from
fleece.

Leave open.

Leave
open.

Seam Line

LEG
Cut 4 from
fleece.

148

SANTA BOTTLE BAG
Instructions are on page 79. Cross-Stitch Cha

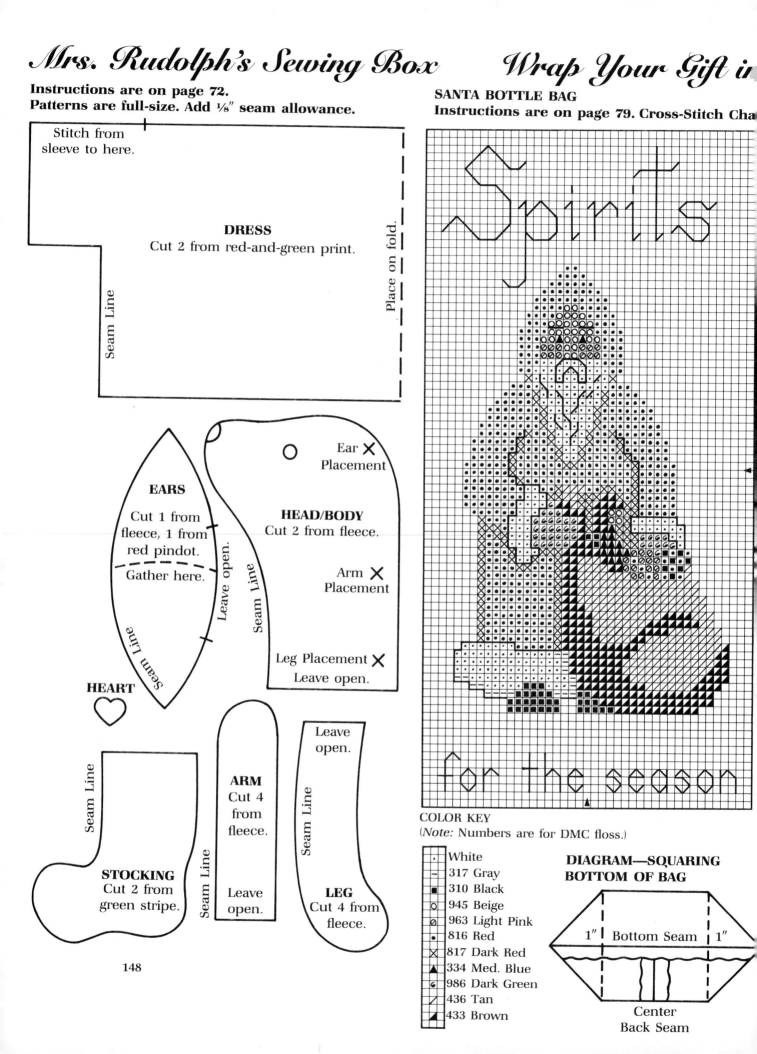

COLOR KEY
(*Note:* Numbers are for DMC floss.)

.	White
−	317 Gray
■	310 Black
O	945 Beige
⊘	963 Light Pink
•	816 Red
✕	817 Dark Red
▲	334 Med. Blue
◓	986 Dark Green
╱	436 Tan
◣	433 Brown

**DIAGRAM—SQUARING
BOTTOM OF BAG**

1"   Bottom Seam   1"

Center
Back Seam

Keepsake Stitchery

SIMMERING SPICE BAG
Instructions are on page 79. Cross-Stitch Chart

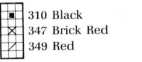

COLOR KEY (*Note:* Numbers are for DMC floss.)

- ■ 310 Black
- ✕ 347 Brick Red
- ╱ 349 Red
- • 352 Coral
- ◢ 580 Medium Green
- s 581 Light Green

With 1 strand, backstitch stems in medium green.

GOLDEN GEESE
Instructions are on page 74.
Patterns are full-size.
Emboss details with dry ballpoint pen.

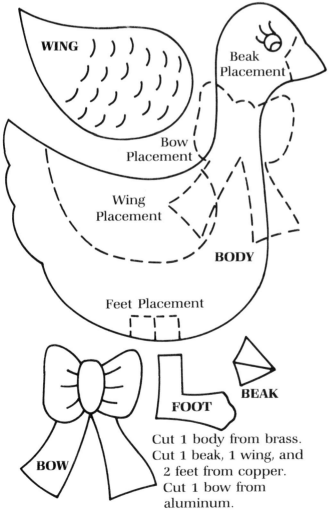

Cut 1 body from brass.
Cut 1 beak, 1 wing, and
2 feet from copper.
Cut 1 bow from
aluminum.

A Flock of Feathered Ornaments

EMBROIDERED QUAIL
Instructions are on page 75.
Pattern is full-size. Add ½″ seam allowance.

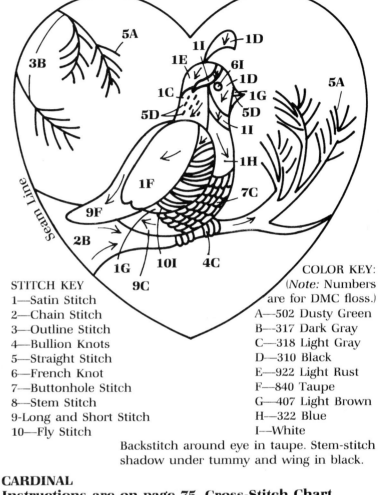

STITCH KEY
1—Satin Stitch
2—Chain Stitch
3—Outline Stitch
4—Bullion Knots
5—Straight Stitch
6—French Knot
7—Buttonhole Stitch
8—Stem Stitch
9-Long and Short Stitch
10—Fly Stitch

COLOR KEY:
(*Note:* Numbers
are for DMC floss.)
A—502 Dusty Green
B—317 Dark Gray
C—318 Light Gray
D—310 Black
E—922 Light Rust
F—840 Taupe
G—407 Light Brown
H—322 Blue
I—White

Backstitch around eye in taupe. Stem-stitch shadow under tummy and wing in black.

CARDINAL
Instructions are on page 75. Cross-Stitch Chart

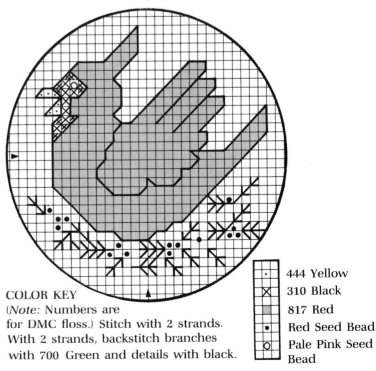

COLOR KEY
(*Note:* Numbers are
for DMC floss.) Stitch with 2 strands.
With 2 strands, backstitch branches
with 700 Green and details with black.

- • 444 Yellow
- ✕ 310 Black
- ▨ 817 Red
- • Red Seed Bead
- ○ Pale Pink Seed Bead

Patchwork Peppermint Duo

Instructions are on page 76.
Patterns are full-size.
Add ¼″ seam allowance to stocking pieces.

Half of pattern. Reverse for other half.

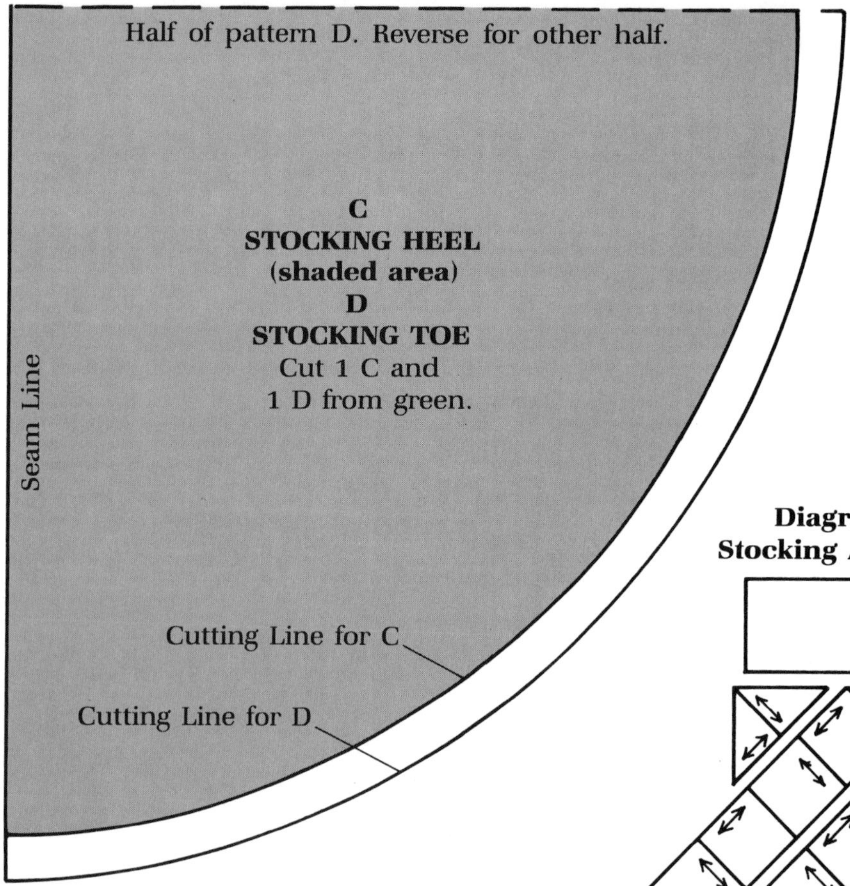

E
STOCKING CUFF
Cut 1 from green.

Seam Line

Half of pattern D. Reverse for other half.

C
STOCKING HEEL
(shaded area)
D
STOCKING TOE
Cut 1 C and
1 D from green.

Seam Line

Cutting Line for C

Cutting Line for D

Diagram—
Stocking Assembly

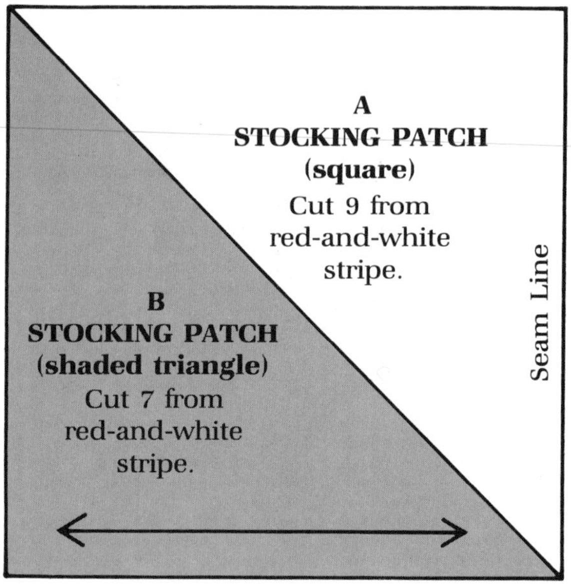

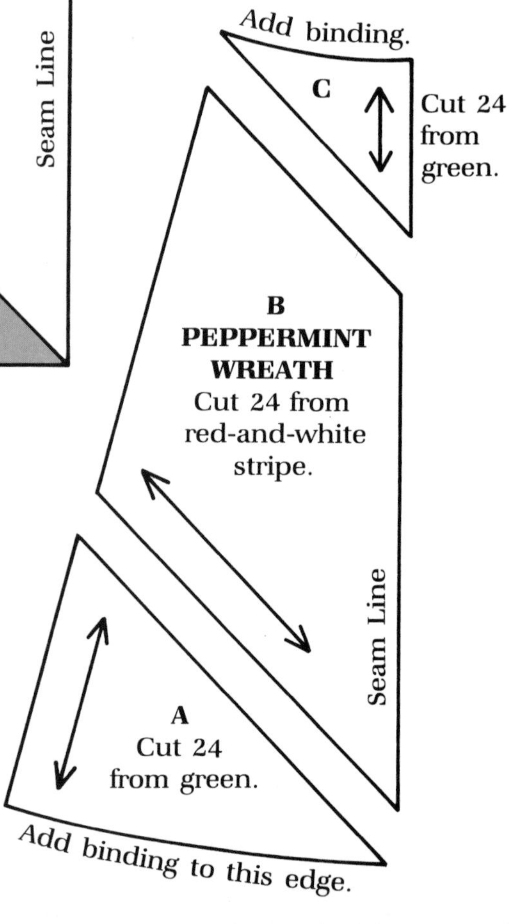

A
STOCKING PATCH
(square)
Cut 9 from
red-and-white
stripe.

B
STOCKING PATCH
(shaded triangle)
Cut 7 from
red-and-white
stripe.

Seam Line

Add binding.

C
Cut 24
from
green.

B
PEPPERMINT
WREATH
Cut 24 from
red-and-white
stripe.

Seam Line

Diagram—Joining Patches
and Wreath Units

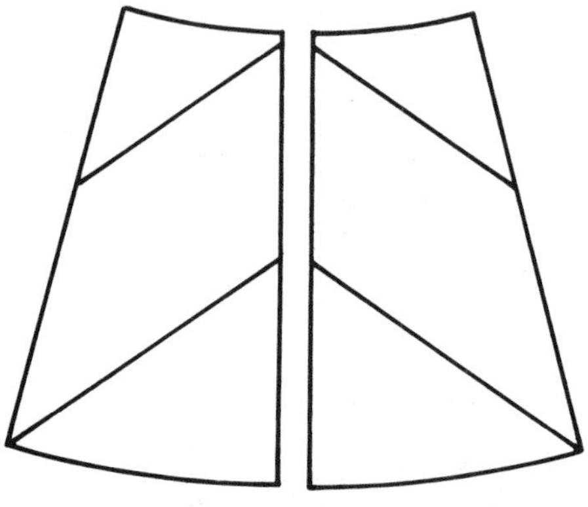

A
Cut 24
from green.

Add binding to this edge.

150

Personal Style: Details that Count

BABY REINDEER
Instructions are on page 89.
Patterns are full-size and include ½″ seam allowance.

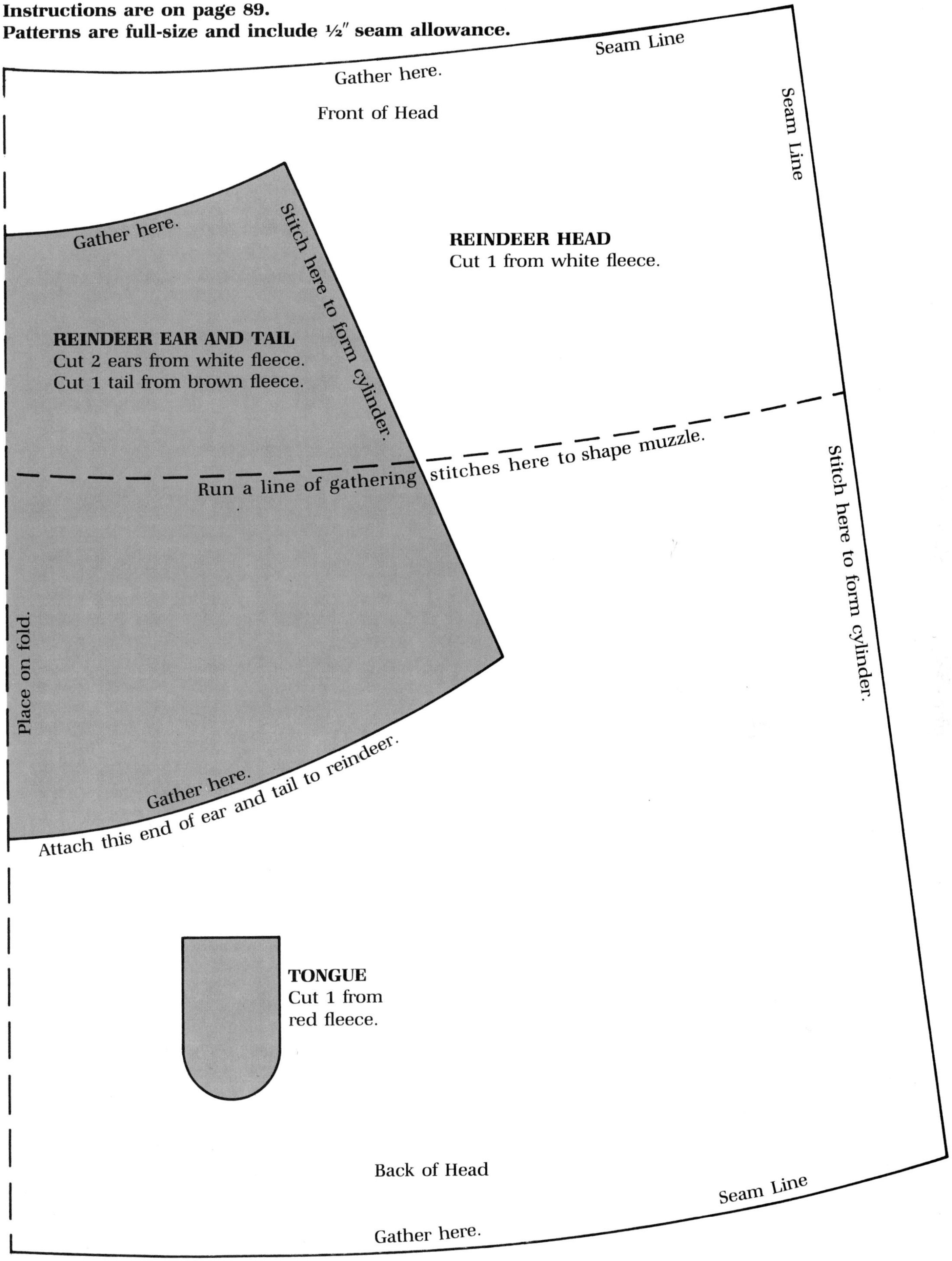

Seam Line

Gather here.

Front of Head

Seam Line

REINDEER HEAD
Cut 1 from white fleece.

Gather here.

Stitch here to form cylinder.

REINDEER EAR AND TAIL
Cut 2 ears from white fleece.
Cut 1 tail from brown fleece.

Run a line of gathering stitches here to shape muzzle.

Stitch here to form cylinder.

Place on fold.

Gather here.

Attach this end of ear and tail to reindeer.

TONGUE
Cut 1 from
red fleece.

Back of Head

Seam Line

Gather here.

Rustic Creations in Wood

**Instructions are on page 81.
Patterns are full-size.**

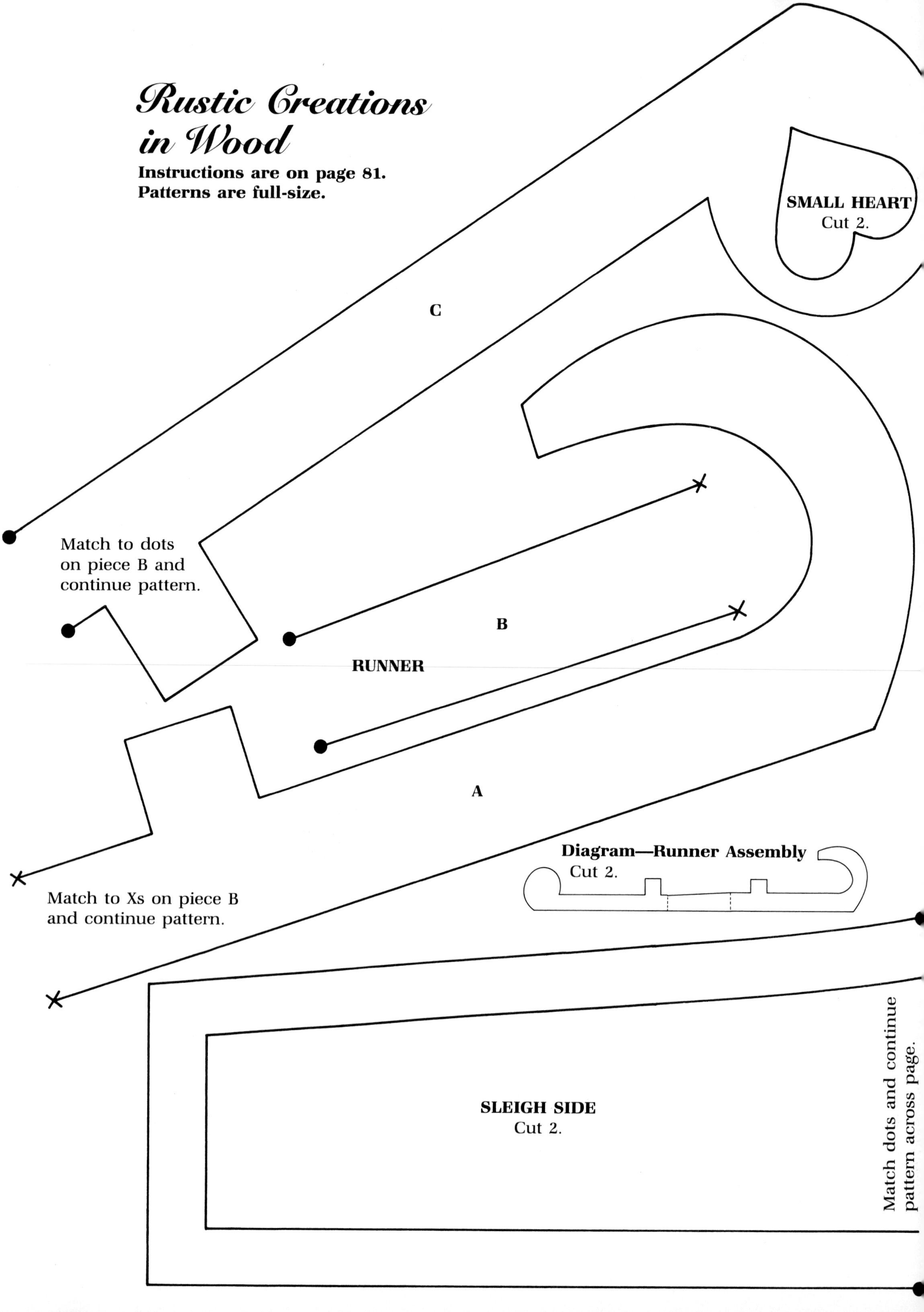

SMALL HEART
Cut 2.

C

Match to dots
on piece B and
continue pattern.

B

RUNNER

Match to Xs on piece B
and continue pattern.

A

Diagram—Runner Assembly
Cut 2.

SLEIGH SIDE
Cut 2.

Match dots and continue
pattern across page.

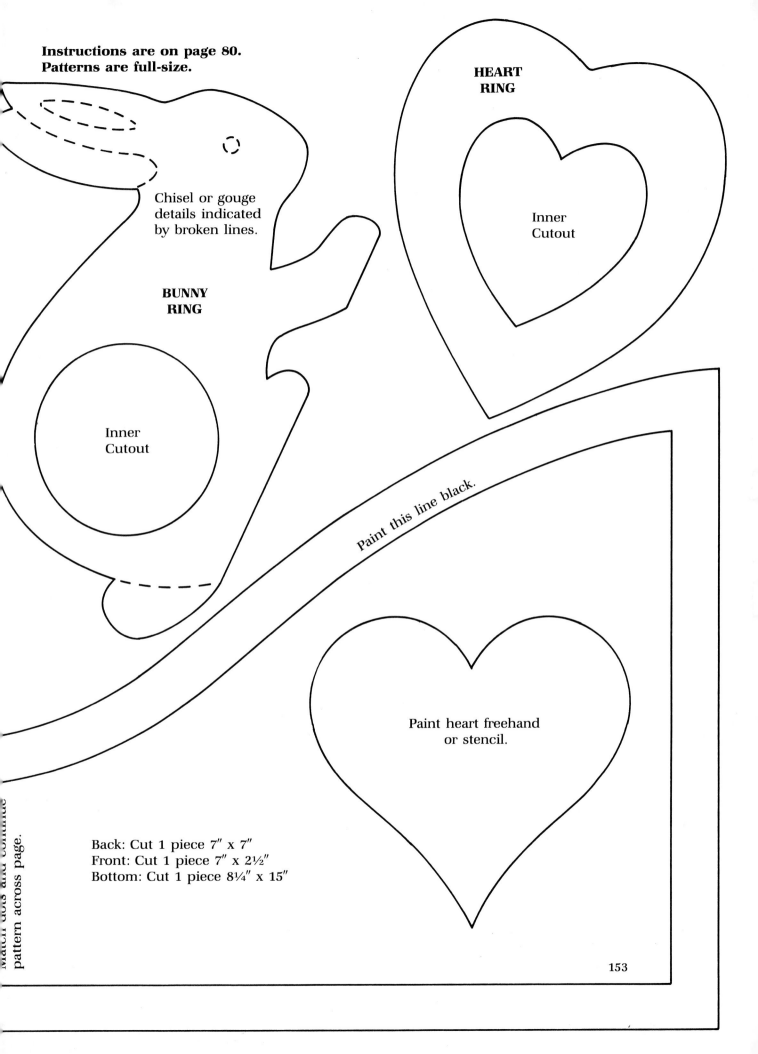

Instructions are on page 80.
Patterns are full-size.

HEART RING

Inner Cutout

Chisel or gouge details indicated by broken lines.

BUNNY RING

Inner Cutout

Paint this line black.

Paint heart freehand or stencil.

Back: Cut 1 piece 7″ x 7″
Front: Cut 1 piece 7″ x 2½″
Bottom: Cut 1 piece 8¼″ x 15″

Match dots and continue pattern across page.

153

Wildlife Stitchery for the Outdoorsman

COLOR KEY

+	729 Medium Old Gold
−	904 Bright Green
○	White
■	310 Black
◢	300 Dark Brown
◿	613 Tan
✕	612 Dark Tan
•	931 Blue

With 1 strand dark tan, backstitch lines on wings and back, around eye, and all outline but tail. With 1 strand black, backstitch tail's outline and details.

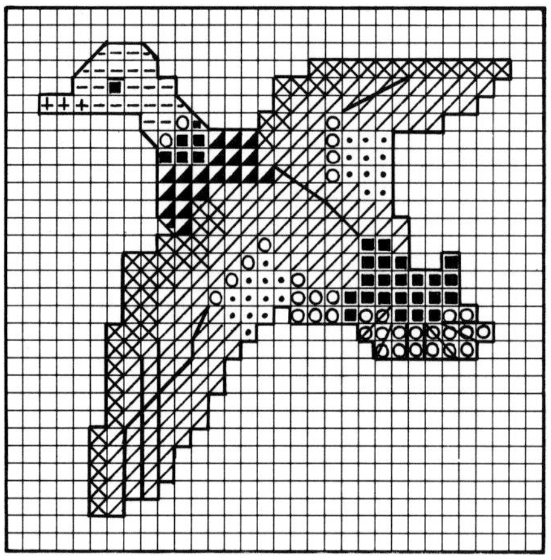

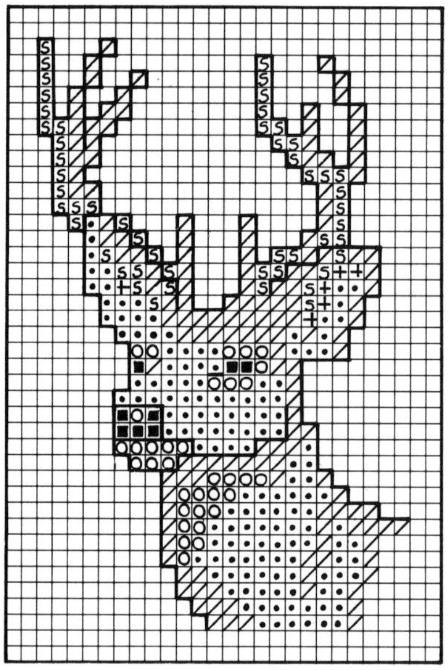

Instructions are on page 87.
Cross-Stitch Chart

COLOR KEY
(*Note:* Numbers are for DMC floss.)

s	632 Dark Brown
◪	732 Golden Brown
•	680 Dark Old Gold
○	White
+	436 Tan
■	310 Black

Backstitch outlines with 1 strand black.

Heavenly Gift Bags

Instructions are on page 94.
Patterns are full-size.
Add ¼″ seam allowance.

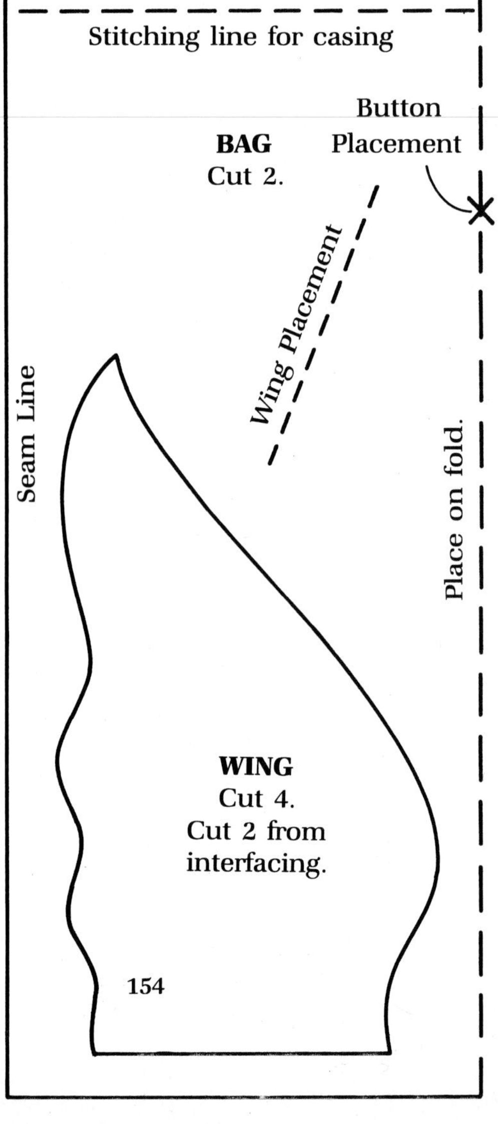

Stitching line for casing

BAG Cut 2.

Button Placement

Wing Placement

Place on fold.

Seam Line

WING Cut 4. Cut 2 from interfacing.

154

Crochet Hearts and Delicate Flowers

Instructions are on page 83.

Next Row

Refer to instructions to work center of runner.

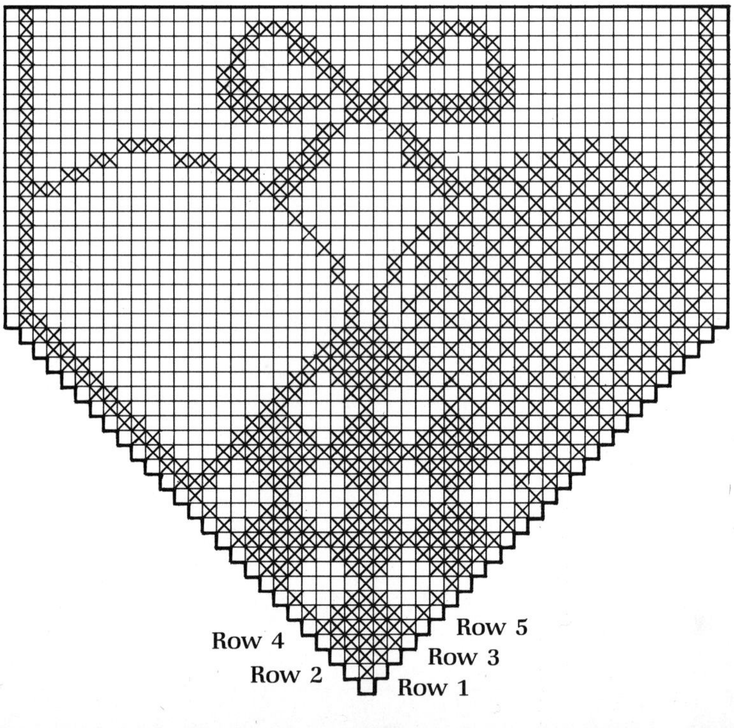

Row 46

Row 4

Row 2

Row 5

Row 3

Row 1

Rc 47

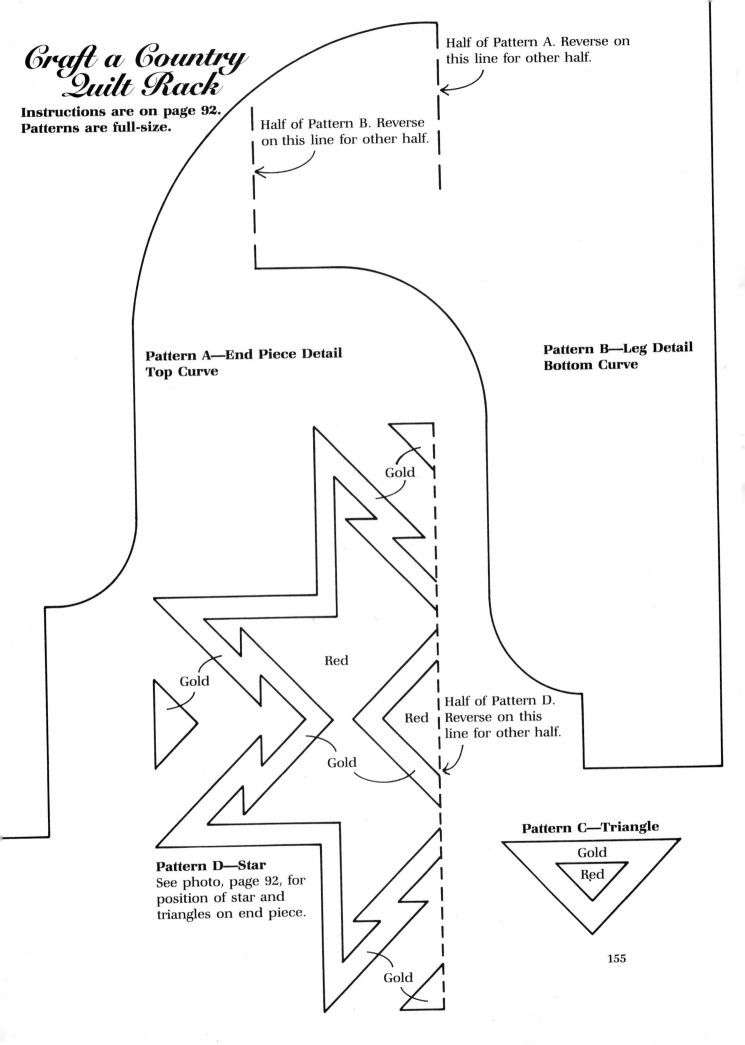

Craft a Country Quilt Rack

**Instructions are on page 92.
Patterns are full-size.**

Half of Pattern A. Reverse on
this line for other half.

Half of Pattern B. Reverse
on this line for other half.

**Pattern A—End Piece Detail
Top Curve**

**Pattern B—Leg Detail
Bottom Curve**

Gold

Gold

Red

Gold

Red

Half of Pattern D.
Reverse on this
line for other half.

Gold

Pattern C—Triangle

Gold

Red

Pattern D—Star
See photo, page 92, for
position of star and
triangles on end piece.

Gold

155

Contributors

DESIGNERS

Sara Jane Ball, gumdrop arrangements, 48, 49, 50.

Mary Martha Blalock, poinsettia tree, top 42.

Teri R. Bond, hair ornaments, 88.

Nena Massey Caldwell, cards and tags, 89.

Pamela Cezayirli, Christmas ribbon tree, 91.

Rebecca Currie, chandelier decorations, 52; peach packages, 52-53.

Lynette Harris Denton, gift wrap, 89.

Becky Dossey, tabletop arrangement, top 40; stairwell arrangement, bottom 40; foyer arrangement, 41.

Lorraine Erwin, wooden napkin rings, 80; sleigh, 81.

Sandra Lounsbury Foose, wreath and stocking, 76.

Barb Griffin, sewing box, 72; Christmas lights sweatshirt and earrings, 60.

Memory E. Hagler, Christmas sweater, 60.

Charlotte Hagood, paper angels, 84.

Cindy Groom Harry, baby reindeer, 88.

Nancy C. Hoerner, simmering spice bag, 78.

Pamela Houk, gingerbread boy garland, 68.

Jo S. Kittinger, wildlife stitchery, 87.

Nancy Marshall, Santa spirits bag, 78.

James D. Murray, Jr., quilt rack, 92.

Karen J. Neuendorf, golden geese, 74.

Kathleen Riley Sharman, mantel decorations, 38-39.

Muriel H. Spencer, cross-stitched cardinal, 75; embroidered quail, 75.

Eunice Svinicki, crocheted table runner and poinsettia, 82.

Carol M. Tipton, paper candlestick garland, 59; cut-paper Nativity, 66; angel gift bags, 94.

The Vanessa-Ann Collection, bell stocking and tree skirt, 56; Christmas memories notebook cover, 64.

Suzanne Wall, peace wall hanging, 70.

Bill Whisenant, wreath, 51.

PHOTOGRAPHERS

Katherine Adams, bottom 42.

Jim Bathie, 43, bottom 78, 94, 96, 97, 98, 101, 102, 105, 106, 109, 111, 112, 115, 118-119, 122, 125, 128, 131, 132, 135.

Van Chaplin, 16, 17, 18, 19.

Gary Clark, 8, 9, 10, 11, 12, 13, 14, 15, 20, 32, 35, 36, 44, 45, 46, 47, 74, top 75, top 78, 81, 82, 83.

Colleen Duffley, cover, title page, contents, 1, 2-3, 21, 22, 22-23, 24, 25, 26, 27, 37, 48, 49, 50, 55, 66, 80, 84, 85, 86, 87, 88, 89, bottom 92, 95.

Mary-Gray Hunter, 51, left 52, 60, 62, 63, 70, 91.

Hal Lott, 38, 39, 40, 41, 54.

Sylvia Martin, top 42, 77.

John O'Hagan, 33, 52-53.

Howard L. Puckett, 73.

Melissa Springer, 56, 57, 59, 65, 68, 69, bottom 75, top 92.

Cheryl Sales, 4, 5, 6, 7, 28, 29, 30, 31.

PHOTOSTYLISTS

Kay Clarke, 43, 78, 96, 97, 98, 101, 102, 105, 106, 109, 111, 112, 115, 118-119, 122, 125, 128, 131, 132, 135.

Connie Formby, 56, 57, 59, 65, 66, 68, 69, 73, bottom 75, 78, 92, 94.

Joetta Moulden, 38, 39, 40, 41, 54.

Houses on pages 38-41 and 54 appeared on Kappa Kappa Gamma Houston Christmas Pilgrimage 1988.

Special thanks to the *Southern Living* Test Kitchens staff for preparing recipes.